three birds
RENOVATIONS

ERIN CAYLESS ♡ **BONNIE** HINDMARSH ♡ **LANA** TAYLOR

murdoch books

Sydney | London

threebirds
RENOVATIONS

Let's make reno magic together!

How it all began ...

'I have no renovating experience and no sense of style ... but I'm IN!'
This was Lana's keen-as-mustard response after receiving a call from Bonnie asking if she wanted to go into business with her and Erin, renovating houses. That's the short story of how Three Birds Renovations began. It literally happened overnight. But our union and eventual success had actually been 15 years in the making – we just didn't know it.

Bon and Ez grew up in the same area and have been best friends since they were teenagers. An unlikely friendship? Perhaps. A case of opposites attracting? Definitely. Bon was a spontaneous, warm, creative extrovert led by the right side of her brain whereas Ez was a self-confessed introvert, a cool as a cucumber left-brained woman who liked to plan everything in advance ... and in writing! If ever there was a case of yin hooking up with yang, this was it.

Their friendship endured through uni, Erin studied human movement and Bon physical education. After this, they put their friendship to the test by job-sharing a role in event management. You might wonder how a job-sharing caper could work with two such different personalities – turns out, pretty great! Their different styles and skills complemented each other perfectly, then and now; Bon designed the creative aspects of the event (in other words, made everything look beautiful) and Ez ran the operational side (i.e. made things actually happen). Little did we know that all of this experience was just a training ground for what was to come. After all, a renovation is pretty much one big event, right?

Then along came Lana in 2002, bursting onto the scene with her larger-than-life personality, loud mouth and all-round sense of fun. She was dating her now-husband, Jason – who Bonnie and Erin worked with, and she quickly completed our trio. If Bon is an extrovert, then Lana is a nextrovert. #nextlevel! Lana hustled away in a fast-paced sales and marketing career after completing her business degree and, as it turns out, her skills were the missing ingredient in the cocktail we were brewing.

First go at working together ... success!

Happy wife, happy life

Even though our work journeys pre-Three Birds were different, our personal lives are almost identical. Erin and Bonnie ended up marrying two guys called Nathan who were also great mates and played in the same footy team with Jason (before he met Lana). #smallworld #ourworld With every new milestone each of us reached, we created a shared life-tapestry unique to the three of us. We've clinked champagne flutes at our hen's parties and lifted each other's wedding dresses in toilet cubicles (as you do). Together, we've celebrated and supported each other through the births of nine children. And, between bubs eight and nine – #surprisebaby4forbon – Three Birds Renovations was born.

Our business was conceived out of a shared desire to turn our backs on the corporate world and build a life we loved. Even though we had the same desire, we were each motivated by different objectives: Erin was looking for a better work/life balance; Lana was in hot pursuit of a new business challenge and Bon was more than ready to live out her lifelong dream of renovating houses for a living.

Of the three of us, Bon was the only one that came close to having any proper reno experience. She had grown up with property-flipping parents, so her family home was always 'under construction'. And just when the dust would settle and everything looked beautiful, they'd sell and she'd move into some new house (aka dump) that was ripe for a reno. So this is in Bon's blood, but even so, there aren't any certificates hanging on her wall. None of us is a qualified architect, interior designer or builder. We don't even have builder-hubbies to turn to. When we started this [ad]venture we had Erin, the calm event manager, Bon, the clever but cautious creative and Lana, the crazily confident marketeer. Individually we didn't have the recipe for success, but together we were unstoppable.

Of course we made mistakes and of course we asked our poor tradies more questions than anybody should be allowed to in a lifetime, but we set out to learn as much as we could, support each other, and get better with each project. And you know what? We have. In four jam-packed years we have renovated nine properties. To break things down a little, that's 32 bedrooms, 18 bathrooms, nine laundries and 11 kitchens – and don't even get us started on decks, extensions, pergolas, pools and gas-strut windows (you'll find out about these beauties on page 85)! Each project has given us the opportunity to learn something new and build our confidence. Everything we know is self-taught and comes from our own real reno experience. Now we're ready to share what we've learned with you.

We designed this book so you can read it in whatever way suits you best. That might mean devouring it cover to cover in one weekend or flicking through a couple of random pages while watching TV or sitting outside the school gates. Each chapter showcases a different home with a collection of our favourite pictures from those projects and our most valuable tips. You'll be able to pick it up and learn something, no matter which page you turn to. Heck, you can even read it in reverse (like Bonnie would) if you'd prefer – it will still make sense.

We hope that you love this book. And we hope it helps you to uncover the opportunities in your own home and get excited about taking them on. But if, for some reason, you never make it past this page, here's our single most important piece of advice:

Life's too short to live in a home you don't love (or at least like). Start thinking about what you could improve in your home today and don't let perfect get in the way of better. If you seek perfection you may never start. Better is better.

Let's do this – together.
Bonnie, Erin and Lana

A cottage with a
modern twist

A *much-loved* family home gets a second life

This fibro cottage had knock-down-rebuild written all over it, but we weren't going to let that happen. We stripped the house back to its bare bones, then gave it a fresh cottage look with weatherboard cladding that would last a lifetime. It was a huge job, but a major win for our budget was spray painting, rather than replacing, the roof. It's quick, cost-effective and the results are incredible!

While the façade felt more like a restoration than a renovation, the back of the house was a completely different story. We built a modern box extension to accommodate a new living room, directly off the open-plan kitchen, and chose to contrast it in every way with the original cottage.

This home will always hold a special place in our hearts. It was owned by the gorgeous Helen Everingham, who tragically lost two sons, Tim and Sam, in a plane crash in 2002. At the time, Sam was Bonnie's long-term partner, and she'd basically grown up in the house. When the opportunity came to buy the home from Helen and save it from being knocked down, we jumped at the chance. Bonnie poured her heart and soul into every aspect of this renovation to bring the home back to life for Sam, his mum and his brother. The house deserved it and they deserved it.

BEFORE

AFTER

Reimagine the floorplan

From the street, you'd never guess what lies behind the front door of this cottage, and we LOVE that element of surprise. This simple extension was totally worth the effort and cost involved. It can be a game changer for an older, more traditional style of house – transforming the way it works for a family.

EXTEND FOR MODERN FAMILY LIFE

Today's families want (and expect) more space and open-plan living than this cottage was able to provide. So we grabbed our pencils and graph paper and hatched a plan for a rectangular extension at the back of the house. The open-plan dining and living room are now connected to the outdoors, and the rooms are so light and spacious. For us, it's the ultimate win-win – a character cottage that ticks all the boxes for modern family living. #jobdone!

DOORS AND WINDOWS MATTER

They have a huge impact on the interior of a home, as well as the exterior, but unfortunately they're often an afterthought; especially when there are more glamorous decisions involving kitchens, flooring or furniture to be made. Long after other items have fallen out of fashion, your windows and doors will endure. So, think of them like Chanel's little black dress – a major investment that will last a lifetime. We guarantee if you don't put time, thought and money into this area, you'll end up kicking yourself later when you realise your doors aren't right and the light, breeze and views you were hoping to enjoy in your new house aren't there because of poorly placed windows.

LIGHT THE OUTDOOR SPACES

While it might make sense to shine a bright spotlight on the lawn and maybe the barbecue area, be careful not to over-light the alfresco areas like the lounging and dining areas where you want to create a mood. Evening wine time is never as enjoyable under supermarket-style lights. Also think about where you will want the light switches to be, and if any of the lights should be on sensors.

MIX YOUR MATERIALS

Don't feel you have to lock yourself into one exterior material for your home. You can combine materials to great effect. In this house we wanted to create a traditional cottage, with a modern twist. On the original cottage we went for a classic weatherboard cladding look, but for the box extension we used ship-lap to clad it vertically and then painted that a dark charcoal. We opted for a different colour on the extension because we wanted it to be a dramatic contrast to the cottage. Depending on your vision you may want to go for a consistent colour or vibe, or break the rules, like we did.

Speak up!

Discuss all of the materials you want to use with your builder. Don't be afraid to be clear and direct about what you want. If you've been dreaming of an exterior clad in weatherboard, make that clear and specify it in their scope of work.

Erin

"There's so much to love about the flow of a house when it has a few steps here and a few steps there. In this house, we converted the original garage into a second living space with an alfresco deck. We connected this extra living space to the main house by adding half a dozen steps. To maintain an open flow, we used the same laminate flooring on both levels, as well as the stairs. We also used bi-fold doors to seamlessly connect the inside and outside."

FLIP TIP

Curb appeal sells houses. No matter what
you do indoors, first impressions count for
a lot, so don't underestimate the wonders
fresh paint, new turf and a few well-chosen
plants can work on a tired exterior.
It's worked a charm for us.

FROM FIBRO TO FAB

If transforming the exterior of the house is high on your wish list, get excited because there are probably more material options than you might realise, and some of the newer products on the market have great benefits in terms of durability and cost. The best material is one that suits the overall look you are going for, is available and can be installed within your timeline, and is one you can afford. Whether you opt for traditional-look weatherboard, modern cladding, brick or brick veneer, you'll find each material has its own pros and cons. For this house, we replaced those old fibro sheets with weatherboard because it was just perfect for that cottage look we were going for.

SAFETY FIRST!

Back in 'the day', a few less-than-safe materials were used in residential builds (lead paint, anyone?). One of these is our old mate, asbestos. Fibro can contain asbestos so always call in licensed professionals to safely remove it. Even though this process costs extra money and can shut down the site for a few days, it's a non-negotiable. #justdoit

GET SOME GABLE IN YOUR LIFE

Also known as 'pitched' or 'peaked' roofs, traditional triangular-shaped roofs like this one include two roof planes and a centre ridge. Roofs like this offer considerable interior space, which can be used for an attic room, or for extra storage. This roof shape also gives you the opportunity to pitch the ceilings inside the home. We LOVE a pitched ceiling inside, so a gabled roof is a real winner in our eyes.

TAKE A CRASH COURSE IN COLOUR

Choosing a colour scheme for the exterior of your home can feel like a pressure test – and we get it, everyone will see it. If you don't trust yourself to pick the best colours first time, search online for inspiration, or explore neighbourhoods to find schemes you like. We fell in love with the grey and white here, and when we added the blush door and those beautiful plants ... it just WORKED!

IF YOU'VE GOT IT, FLAUNT IT

Part of the reason this exterior works so well is because we've called out the quaint cottagey details by painting them crisp white, creating contrast, interest and symmetry. We also toned down the appearance of the gutters and downpipes by painting them the same grey as the house, which makes them much less noticeable.

TEST DRIVE BEFORE YOU BUY

We never paint a house without painting big test swatches (always two coats). Paint any trim colours you're considering around those swatches to get a feel for how the two colours will look together. Let the paint dry completely, then check it out at different times of day as the light changes.

WORK YOUR WAY DOWN

As we mentioned on page 14, one of the biggest wins for the budget on this house was spray painting the roof rather than replacing it. If you are able to go this route too, we recommend you tackle the roof BEFORE you start any other exterior work. That includes painting, cladding and installing doors. The reason we say this is that a roof needs to be properly cleaned and prepped before it's painted, and the first time we had this done, we could not believe the amount of black gunk that came off the roof. Years of crusted black nastiness came flying off the roof in all directions and it was not pretty. Trust us, you don't want that stuff anywhere near your beautiful fresh paint or new weatherboard cladding. Tackle any exterior jobs from the top down, and then thank us later!

Door furniture!

DON'T FORGET DOOR FURNITURE

'Door what'? 'Door furniture' – that's the fancy name used to describe door handles and locks. We're guessing door handles are pretty far down your wish list. In fact, we're willing to bet our door furniture budget that door handles aren't even on your radar. Let this serve as a reminder to make sure you give this detail the same amount of thought that you give every other detail of your reno. If you don't tell your builder what door handles you want, you'll arrive home one day to find the decision has been made for you – opportunity missed! And trust us, you want a major say in what door handles get installed as they can make a big difference to how a door looks. Case in point, the gorgeous gold front door handle and lock are the cherries on top of this dusty pink door.

MAKE A STATEMENT

The entrance to your home is a wonderful opportunity to signpost your style, and a beautiful door doesn't have to break your budget. This pink door is probably one of our most popular. And guess what? It was cheap as chips from the local hardware store. Front doors can even be considered fast fashion – there's no reason why they can't be updated with a new coat of paint every season. A fresh-looking front door, particularly if it's a coloured one, can really make your house stand out from the crowd. The colour of this door and the gold of the handle work so well with the pretty outdoor lights that frame the door. And again, these didn't cost much, but they look amazing and make a big impact.

Island life

Aim for 1200 mm between your main wall and your island, although when space is tight you can get away with a minimum of 900 mm. Island benches should be between 800 and 1200 mm wide and as long as your space allows. This island bench is only 800 mm wide.

IDENTIFY YOUR KITCHEN VIBE

Right from the start, we wanted this kitchen to be a room that felt relaxing – a place where the owners would feel grounded and inspired. We knew achieving this was going to come down to choosing the right materials and colours. Pale green cabinetry, marble-look Caesarstone, gold and silver finishes, lots of greenery and flowers and light-coloured flooring gave us the exact feeling we were hoping for. Green (in any shade) is growing in popularity and will continue to do so. It's a nod to nature and, when used in its palest form, feels fresh and calming. There are so many examples of this colour working well – in both a modern and retro setting. Because we were keeping the kitchen open, we decided to forgo overhead cabinetry for a floating shelf to display pretty things. We also designed an island

with legs on it, to make it look more like a beautiful piece of furniture. There is no one thing that makes this kitchen work, it's the combination of colours, textures, layout and cabinet style that creates the magic and flow.

CABINET COLOURS GALORE!

Today's colour-matching technology means you can quite literally have your polyurethane cabinets painted to match any colour you desire. And if you're desperate for a sea-change down the track, you can have them resprayed!

Of *all* the renovations we've done, this *green* kitchen is still one of our *favourites*.

APPLIANCE SCIENCE

Big-ticket items like ovens, dishwashers and fridges should never be an impulse purchase. We understand that shopping for them can be overwhelming – there are so many options and you're not outlaying a small amount of cash. On top of that, you have to select them very early in your reno because they impact your entire kitchen design. In fact, it's fair to say that – depending on your needs and choices – your kitchen may end up being designed around your appliances. That's a lot of pressure to get things right! But take time to really think things through – take lots of measurements and play around with the kitchen layout and the scale of the appliances until you feel sure you've got something that will really work for you.

INTEGRATE YOUR APPLIANCES

Because this kitchen was part of a larger living space and we wanted the kitchen to flow seamlessly into the areas around it, we integrated all the appliances to make it look less 'kitcheny'. A common misconception is that integrated appliances are difficult to repair and replace. Our kitchen guy tells us this is not the case and he makes a good point that if you buy quality appliances, they should pretty much last through to your next kitchen reno anyway.

CUPBOARDS OR DRAWERS?

This is a common dilemma but it shouldn't be. The ideal solution is quite simple: below waist height, drawers reign supreme! The only exception to this is under the sink and in a floor-to-ceiling food pantry with shallow shelves. Most kitchens will likely have a combination of drawers and cupboards. Your budget may also impact your choice, as drawers are generally more expensive. If flipping for profit, go with the minimum number of drawers you can get away with.

KEEP YOUR ISLAND BENCH CLEAR

We mean completely clear, with NOTHING on it at all (except perhaps one luxe soap dispenser if you're a big hand-washer like Lana #germaphobe). Having a zero tolerance policy for clutter on your island means you simply won't accumulate stuff there. We're not talking about food prep and plates, which of course will cover your island daily. We mean don't 'style' the island with things that sit there permanently, like books, bowls and other decorative items. Your island is a workspace that's going to be used daily, so it should be totally clear at the start of every day and totally clear at the end (we're talking ideal world here!).

HOW HIGH TO HANG PENDANTS?

This question is super important! There's nothing worse than pendants hung at the wrong height (and by that, we mean they're usually too high). That's why we leave this important moment til the styling phase of our reno, after the island is installed. That way, Bon can use her eye to help get the pendants at the right height. Most electricians don't like doing it this way. They'd prefer to install them during the reno while they're on site doing other things and they can make lots of mess without getting into trouble. But without the visual reference of the island bench to help, you run the risk of the pendants being hung at the wrong height. So, if you can wait, do! As a rule of thumb, we like to hang our pendants somewhere between 700 and 850 mm above the benchtop (that's to the base of the pendant). If you're a tall person, maybe go a bit higher, and if the pendants are clear glass, you can go a bit lower, if you prefer. It is essential that you make decisions about lighting early in your reno so your builder and electrician can prepare the ceiling cavity and 'rough in' the electricals. Bear in mind that while the height of your pendants can be adjusted at the styling stage, the location of them cannot.

MULTIPLE SEATING OPTIONS

Everyone loves lounging on a sofa, but we always include additional seating options. These don't necessarily have to be traditional lounge chairs – sturdy furniture that can double as a side table, stools or an ottoman can also be great choices. A bench-seat picture window, like the one we installed here, is also a firm fave of ours.

Juju hats
ADD SOFTNESS

RUG LIFE

We don't follow many rules when it comes to choosing rugs, we're rebels at heart, but we always invest in quality. In other words, buy the best rug you can afford. Sometimes we use a large rug that frames the space and fits under the sofa. Other times, we layer two rugs on top of each other. Buy a rug that's big enough to fit under the legs of at least the main sofa, preferably the occasional chairs too. Many stores will let you take a rug home to test it out, so it's worth asking.

WE LOVE AN OCCASIONAL CHAIR

As their name suggests, they're only used occasionally as the sofa is usually the first choice for people to park their butts. These chairs are a little fancier, and a great way to introduce some extra style and interest to a room. You can get single chairs that match your sofa exactly but we tend to lean towards mixing things up with different occasional chairs.

GREENERY

We look for plant and pot combos at the exact height our room needs. Plants bring a relaxed feel to a lounge room and we sometimes opt for faux versions; they're especially handy for flip properties when we're not around to water them.

LAST, BUT DEFINITELY NOT LEAST, DON'T OVER-LIGHT THE ROOM

You don't want to live your life under the glare of supermarket-style lights indoors, especially in living areas that don't need it. Warm white globes and dimmers are your friends, particularly for those occasions where a darker ambience is called for, like dinner parties. They're also great in a baby's nursery for night-time feeds.

Finding the right art for your colour scheme can be tricky, because art is so subjective. But, at a basic level, ask yourself whether you want a piece that contrasts or complements your colour scheme. In this dining room we had a blush theme going on, so we chose artwork that worked with that.

COLOURED COUCHES

When choosing couches, we will be guided by the overall look we're trying to achieve, but we can go one of two ways: a neutral colour (grey, cream or white) or a pop of colour that makes a statement. Certainly, a neutral is the fail-safe option and it's hard to go wrong with a pale grey sofa. But then we seem to always find a way to make a pop of colour work just as well. We'd avoid a sofa with a print or a pattern. Stick with a solid colour and bring in patterns through your cushions and rugs.

WALL CANDY

There's nothing more boring than a blank space above a sofa. #snoozefest! That's why we always include a bit of wall candy in our lounge rooms. If you have a big empty space to fill, lucky you! This is a great opportunity to add some interest and tell a story. The options are endless; you can go for a large mirror, to bounce light around and make the room seem bigger, or for bold and bright art that makes an instant statement. A large print in muted tones that tie in with other elements in the room can also be a great choice. Choosing artwork doesn't need to be daunting and remember, wall art doesn't necessarily have to mean a painting or a print, it can be a soft-textured item like a juju hat or a gorgeous woven macramé hanging.

CUSHION CRUSH

Oh, we love us a good cushion. You'll notice we tend to pick a hero cushion that provides a pop of colour, and then one or two that add texture, and a few more to complement the colour tones in the room. The complementary cushions might vary in pattern but they always work together so the overall effect is not too busy.

Show some leg

In a small space, showing more leg (sofa leg, that is) helps to create the illusion of a bigger room because you can see the floor continuing under the sofa. This same theory applies to bathroom vanities – we like to mount those on the wall to create space underneath them.

Room to play! ♡

ADD BEDROOMS TO YOUR HIT LIST

Even if you aren't doing a whole-home reno, bedrooms should still make the cut for a makeover as they're one of the easiest spaces to refresh and renew. Because they're confined areas, they don't need to be designed with the adjacent rooms in mind, unlike the kitchen or living/dining rooms. You can create your own vibe in a bedroom – one that's unique to you. If you choose to locate one of your bedrooms away from the others (perhaps a guest room or a teenager's bedroom), make sure there's a toilet nearby to service it.

IT'S HARD TO GO PAST CARPET

As much as we love floorboards, we can't deny the feel-good factor of carpet in bedrooms. We wouldn't do a whole house in wall-to-wall carpet, but a bedroom? Definitely. Who doesn't love waking up in the morning and putting their feet on a lovely, soft surface rather than a cold, hard floor? Enough said. But carpet can stain, which makes it hard work if you have pets, kids or red wine drinkers in the household. And yep, you can choose fabrics and brands that are more stain-resistant than others, but there's only so much they can withstand.

AN EASY UPDATE FOR KIDS' ROOMS

We love how often rugs pop up as a styling solution. It's because they're just so damn versatile. Once we've got a super-soft carpet down, we like to layer that up with a rug or two to encourage playtime on the floor. Rugs on top of carpet are a winner for adding texture and interest. And they can be easily updated as your kids grow to make the room look and feel more grown up.

SKIP THE BEDHEAD

There's no question that the area above a bed can handle a lot of drama. Bedheads look amazing, but a bed frame or a fancy bedhead can set you back some serious coin, so don't feel you need one in order to create a luxurious look. A beautiful piece of art above the bed can have just as much impact. Choose a piece that works with the overall theme and mood of the room you want to create. If you need to save cash, an ensemble of Euro pillows and artwork can be used to create a feature in the bedroom (see page 126). This is especially relevant when staging a property for sale. There's no need to invest in a bedhead.

LAYER UP FOR DIMENSION

Nothing looks sadder than a bed with just a sheet and two pillows. We see it on Airbnb all the time and we always wonder if the owners realise how many more enquiries they'd get if that bed had some layers #moreismore. Layers make any bedroom look more multidimensional and feel cosier. So be generous with your bedding – we suggest 2 doonas (for that extra fluffy look) + 4 pillows (a combo of Euro and standard) + 3 decorative cushions + 1 throw or blanket for the end of the bed. Each layer needs to work with the overall colour palette of the room. Look for opportunities to add texture to the bed rather than just colour. This could be through introducing a chunky knit blanket or embellished sequined cushion.

LINEN CRUSH!

We love cotton, but give us linen sheets any day of the week and thrice on 'sleep-in Sundays'! Linen is luxurious and more affordable these days. Not only does it get softer the more you wash it, linen also has that slightly rumpled look that's relaxed, inviting and more forgiving on those mornings of slap-dash bed-making when you're trying to get ready for the day.

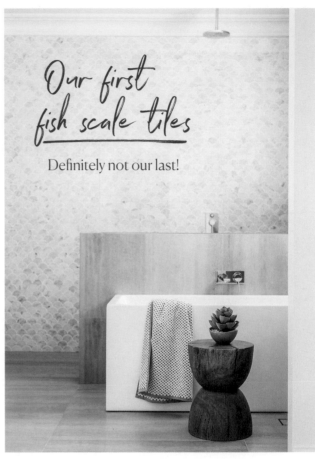

Our first fish scale tiles

Definitely not our last!

GO BOLD WITH THE BATH

This black bath was the first item Bonnie chose for this bathroom, so we kept the other design elements quite muted to allow the bath to really pop. Most baths range in size from 1400–1800 mm long and about 850 mm wide, but avoid the temptation to wedge the biggest bath you can fit into the space. If you've got 2000 mm to work with, that's not a green light to squeeze an 1800 mm freestanding bath in there. They need a bit of breathing room – 200 mm at either end is a good amount. Never push a freestanding bath hard up against a wall, even on the long side under the tap (unless it's designed to sit flush with the wall, that is – like the one on page 71). Aim to keep it 100 mm away from the wall. If you can't give a freestanding bath the necessary breathing space, go for a built-in (like Bon did on page 194).

FREESTANDING BATHS: THE CONS

There's nowhere to put soap or a glass of wine (hey, we aren't judging), so you'll need a stool or a well-placed wall niche. They also have high sides, making them challenging for kiddies or nanna to get in and out of. Some are also super heavy, so flooring may need to be reinforced. Finally, they can be tricky to clean behind. But all is forgiven when they look this good!

BIG TILES AND SLABS ARE HOT!

They produce fewer grout lines, are easier to clean and create a more seamless look. But they can make it harder for your tiler to manipulate the fall (particularly in small bathrooms). You may need an expensive strip drain to cover more floor area. #worthit!

FLIP TIP

Your bathroom should appeal to the masses, so this isn't the time to go crazy with colours and pattern that might polarise buyers. Play it safe with neutrals and a marble look. You can always add colour through styling.

WE LOVE A TIMBER BENCHTOP

They bring warmth to a space, are easy to install and can be a great money saver when they're from places like IKEA. They need oiling with water-resistant oil before using, but this isn't hard. When we first started out, oiling the timber benchtops for our renos became Erin's DIY specialty. Just be careful not to accidentally buy particle board (like we did once) as that won't handle water. You're after a solid piece of timber.

TAILOR YOUR LAUNDRY TO YOU

Who doesn't want a clear bench to fold clothes on? It makes the task of folding that little bit more bearable. Keep this in mind when you're designing your laundry area, and don't forget to think about how many items you'll be putting on that valuable bench space – a washing basket, for example. Will you still have enough room to fold clothes once that's on the bench? If not, give yourself enough cupboard storage and shelving to store items off the benchtop. Obviously, you have to work with the space you've got, but you can maximise your bench space by opting for under-bench appliances. A front-loader washing machine (instead of a top-loader) will provide you with an extra 800 mm of bench space. Wall-mounted taps will also give you a little bit of extra space. Depending on your priorities, you could opt for a half-width sink to free up more workspace and/or go for a fitted sink cover to turn your tub into even more folding space.

Double doors!
They make this laundry more inviting.

Hamptons
in the hills

Our six-week *wonder!*

Even though this reno was our second, it was twice as challenging as the first flip because the house was in OK condition and could be lived in immediately. In fact, the kitchen had been recently renovated, so adding substantial value in just six weeks was going to be a huge challenge for us.

We saw the potential in this house straight away and knew a few simple changes could be really effective. The exterior was very beige and bland with blonde brick, unloved cladding and ugly block-out shutters that looked like they hadn't been raised in years. We saw opportunities to improve the house everywhere we turned, but especially out the back where we found a random brick room that looked like a garage but led to nowhere (according to the real estate brochure this was the 'alfresco zone'!). We knew we could make a huge change there.

As with all our renovations, we wanted to transform ugly into beautiful, closed-off into connected, and dark into light. It's a cliché, but we really did want to create the house of our dreams. Consequently, we agonised over every decision – from big ones like where to put the fourth bedroom, to smaller ones, like whether to have handles or knobs on the kitchen cabinets. It all paid off. Our goal was to create a house that would give people a wonderful feeling when they walked through it, and we definitely achieved that. The true test of each house we renovate is to ask ourselves one simple question: Would we want to live here? If the answer is yes, we're happy!

BEFORE

AFTER

Bonnie

"It's amazing what a crisp white balustrade can do for your street appeal! It's my absolute go-to for transforming a façade, and I usually remove unruly shrubs at the same time. Don't get me wrong, I love greenery, but there's a time and place for it – you don't want it covering your house or making everything look and feel smaller and darker."

THE OUTDOOR CONNECTOR

The ideal alfresco area doesn't just give you another liveable space outside, it connects the indoors to the outdoors. In other words, if you have options as to where to put your alfresco space (at the front, side or back of your house), first and foremost your priority should be to create a seamless flow from the main living area of the house to the outside space. We love positioning alfresco areas off the kitchen whenever we can. And, to test whether or not we've cracked that seamless flow we're looking for, we use our patented (not really) Three Birds outdoor connector test: can you pass something – say, a sandwich or jug of Pimm's – from your kitchen to someone in the alfresco space? If you can, winner! You've successfully completed the first important step to creating that connection.

OUTDOOR TRANSFORMATION

When we bought this house, the real estate brochure described this dark, cold space as the 'alfresco space'. (Umm, they're joking, right?) We were able to add major value in this area by knocking down those walls, ripping off the roof and building a simple pergola. We added a gas strut window and timber servery, and some French doors from the kitchen to really make this an outdoor area to be proud of (rather than terrified by).

PAVING PAINT TO THE RESCUE

We love paving paint! It can turn an ugly, old concrete pathway or pool surround into a fresh footway in no time. It's super-easy to apply so you can even do it yourself. We also love using paving paint in alfresco spaces where tiling is too expensive. Just add an outdoor rug and some fresh furniture and no-one will ever notice the absence of tiles. Best of all, paving paint is easy on the wallet.

FLIP TIP

Outdoor rugs are so useful when styling a house for sale. They're perfect for disguising a boring (and probably cracked) concrete porch. Our MO is usually to refresh the concrete with paving paint and then throw a rug down. You can even cheat a little by using an indoor rug to style the outdoor space as you'll only be putting it out for a few hours during the open homes.

BEFORE

AFTER

Timber touches

Kitchens can be hard and angular spaces. Leaning a couple of timber chopping or cheese boards in different shapes and sizes against the splashback introduces some texture and warmth. We love round boards for this reason.

Big results
on a small budget.

THIS FLAT-PACK KITCHEN
WAS A WINNER FOR US.

TACKLING THE HEART OF THE HOME

A kitchen reno can be one of the most challenging because it's the heart of the home. Even if you're not going to be a MasterChef contender any time soon, your kitchen still constitutes a major part of your overall space, so it should look good and function well. And sure, there are ways to renovate a kitchen on a small budget, but even then it's still likely to end up being one of the most expensive rooms in your home, so you need to be happy with the end result. As if that wasn't pressure enough, you've probably heard the expression 'kitchens sell houses' ... so this is a real reno moment and a golden opportunity to add some serious value to your home. #kachingkaching

We designed this kitchen to be a destination zone within the house. It was originally located in the middle of a long room, making it more of a thoroughfare rather than a place the family wanted to spend time in. It needed to be an open, breezy space that invited people to take a seat. By relocating the entire kitchen to the end of the long room, we created a new alfresco zone directly off the kitchen. With its custom-built breakfast bar and gas-strut window, that new entertaining space was fully integrated into the kitchen. The finishing touch was a pair of French doors leading directly out to the pool, giving Mum and Dad a perfect view of the kids from the kitchen.

PICK UP A FLAT-PACK KITCHEN

Who doesn't love a custom-made cabinet? People on a tight budget, that's who! If you're on a budget, flat-pack cabinetry might just be your new best friend. We've installed some amazing flat-pack kitchens and laundries in our houses, and saved big money in the process. This kitchen renovation was a hybrid; the previous owners had already attempted a kitchen reno using a flat-pack kit, so when we bought the property, we re-used the cabinetry already there and added to it with the same brand of flat-pack. It looked great, saved us a pretty penny and helped to make this flip one of our most profitable!

HIRE SOME HELP

Whether you're installing a flat-pack kitchen in a flipped home or a forever home, we recommend you hire a carpenter to put it together. Yes, it's an extra cost, but overall you'll save loads of time (and, even better, you'll save your sanity).

Swap old metal pool fences for glass where it counts.

AND ENJOY UNINTERRUPTED WATER VIEWS. #YESPLEASE!

If money is tight, timber benchtops can be a great cost saver in the kitchen.

AND THEY STILL LOOK SO GOOD!

USE WHITE TO SHOWCASE THE GREEN

If you're lucky enough to have some lush greenery outside a window, it's probably worth showing off. And the most effective way to do this is by creating a white-out inside. If everything is light and neutral inside, the green outside will really pop.

The power of white paint!

REFRESH RATHER THAN REBUILD YOUR STAIRCASE

Just because a staircase is practical, doesn't mean it has to be boring! Stairs can have a huge impact on how your home looks, feels and functions. And just because a staircase is fabulous, doesn't mean it has to break the bank. Before you rip out your old staircase, try refreshing it with a new coat of paint. The dark feature wall here was the perfect colour to hide that Swedish-sauna timber panelling. Once complete, that colour also provided the perfect backdrop for the pure white staircase. This was all done in one weekend.

BEFORE

AFTER

Lana

"It's really important to road test your new bathroom layout (or the layout of any room for that matter!). To work out what your new layout might look and feel like, try marking it on the floor using masking tape. You can also pin up bed sheets to represent new walls, or stack up boxes as a pretend bath or vanity. Move around inside your new layout to see if you like how it feels, and if the proportions seem right. Soak it all in!"

CLEANSE YOUR SOUL, NOT JUST YOUR TEETH

The smoothest bathroom renos are the ones where all the planning and design work has been done upfront – nice and early! Bathrooms are complex little beasts to renovate. Things need to be done in a very specific order, so you can't change your mind halfway through if you come up with a better idea. (Well, technically you can, but it will cost you time, money and your tradies' patience.) Put the hard yards in early and nut out the finer details in order to give yourself the best chance of getting what you want – tiles and grout colour, taps, toilets, vanities, bathtubs, shower screens, waste placement, lighting … the list goes ON! Remember, if you don't know what you want, your builder, plumber or tiler will decide for you. And take it from us, they don't always have the best design ideas. #gulp

DON'T FEAR THE SKINNY ENSUITE

It can actually be a designer's delight where the vanity can be the star of the show, with the toilet neatly hidden up one end and a deep walk-in shower at the other. It's a nice combo, providing privacy while still feeling open. You'll also save on glazier costs with no shower screen to deal with.

THIS PROPERTY DIDN'T HAVE SPACE FOR A POWDER ROOM

It didn't have room for a guest bathroom either, so we turned this laundry into a dual-purpose laundry/powder room. If you decide to go this route in your home, our golden rule is to tuck the toilet behind the bench, or out of plain view so your guests feel some sense of privacy despite being in what is technically a laundry. You'll also need to think about where to place a mirror, as this will make the room feel more like a bathroom than a laundry. A pretty sink, tapware and pendant light also go a long way to making sure your guests don't feel they're in a utilitarian laundry. Oh, and one more thing ... make sure there's a lock on the door!

FLIP TIP

If you're staging an open house and want to get top dollar, it's a good idea to showcase the laundry area at its best – that means making sure you've got at least a washing machine in the space. But don't spend any money plumbing in a washing machine. In fact, it doesn't even need to work, it just needs to be there.

Santorini
in Sydney

Lana's *forever* home

Having lived in this house for 15 years, Lana knew she was finally ready to renovate her home, even though she had no idea what style to go with. Hamptons? Scandi? Coastal? Boho? ... She liked them all!

When envisioning your dream home, it's awesome to dream BIG, but you also don't want to be off with the fairies. You've got to work with what you've got! By that we mean you have to look at the features and bones of your home and try to imagine them as a better version of themselves. That's what Lana was eventually able to do with her Forever Home.

Truth be told, it took her a pretty while to pick up on the Tuscan vibes the terracotta-coloured render and climbing bougainvillea were emitting. But, once she tuned into them, the penny dropped and Lana realised the best renovation for her home was going to be one that embraced its distinctly Euro origins. After a lot of vision boarding (a process we teach in The Reno School), she finally landed on the idea of a modern Mediterranean villa, or, as it's more affectionately known around Three Birds HQ, #santoriniinsydney.

Once her vision was nailed down, the rest of the design decisions were a breeze. We had an answer for everything. Lana's vision board became our true north and her terracotta house became the whitewashed family home of her dreams.

BEFORE

AFTER

Any old pots get a makeover

Before you buy any pots, look for old ones lying around
your garden, then paint them to match your house using the
same paint as the exterior, like we did here.

Lana

GET REAL ABOUT YOUR BIG VISION

Before you fall in love with a vision for your dream home, do a bit of research so you understand the original architectural style of the home you have, as this should guide you on what 'looks' may be easiest to achieve. For example, if your house is a 1920s Californian bungalow, you're probably best renovating to a style that works with some of the original features of that home rather than trying to create something completely different. With Lana's home, the original Tuscan render made it easy to create a modern Mediterranean-style look – it just worked. If, however, her dream had been to have a Federation-style home with fretwork and a wrap-around balcony … well, no amount of renovating would have made that happen because her house just didn't have Federation origins. To put it another way, if you're born with the same colouring as Nicole Kidman or Naomi Watts, you'll be forever disappointed if you keep showing inspo pictures of Eva Mendes to your hairdresser. The same goes for houses. Work with what you've got and improve on it.

GIVE IT UP FOR CONCRETE ROOF TILES!

Lana replaced her terracotta roof tiles with concrete ones and reckons they're a winner on every front. Not only are they cheaper than terracotta tiles, concrete roof tiles also happen to be the most durable and economical option on the market – they actually strengthen with age and can last up to 50 years. (Believe us, not many things get better with age when it comes to renovating!) They are made from sand and cement, usually with a pigmented coat on top or mixed through for longer wear. They're unglazed too, so it's easier to change the colour of your roof down the track. Concrete tiles are pretty much the chameleons of the roof tile world as they can be created to resemble many other styles and materials.

"Plan your window coverings, both inside and out. External shutters can bring your vision to life and provide accent colour, while your choice of internal window coverings can also be seen from the street."

PAINT IS YOUR FRIEND

If you already live in a rendered or 'bagged' house (bagging is a lighter, easier version of rendering), a fresh coat of paint and change of colour might be all you need to transform the exterior. Lana loved her bagged home, but wasn't in love with the terracotta colour, so she painted it using Dulux Weathershield in Casper White Quarter and nailed that Greek-island look.

THE MUST-HAVE MUD ROOM

The concept of a mud room is nothing new. In fact, mud rooms are a staple in homes located in wet, cold and country areas. This is Lana's 'urban mud room' – a place to put shoes on and take them off, and maintain her white-on-white Santorini style. Seriously, no-one gets past this room with their shoes on (except the police – they refused, but that's a story for another book!). Regardless of where you live, if you can fit a mud room in your home, it's a winner for tossing school bags, hats, dirty shoes and all those items you walk through the front door carrying. Ideally, this room should be located wherever you enter the house, either just inside the front door, or next to your garage if you have internal access.

HOLY MOTHER OF STAIRCASES!

At least that's what we thought when we saw this 10-metre wonder spring to life in Lana's Forever Home. This one proves that staircases can connect levels AND take your breath away at the same time. Lana wanted her stairs to be an architectural feature – a functional piece of art. Supported by a powder-coated steel frame, the stairs look as if they're floating mid-air and have a seamless finish. There are no fussy supports or busy balustrades to distract the eye from the stunning zig-zag design created by the boxed-in treads and risers. There was a lot of debate about whether to leave them unpainted, with a timber finish, but Lana had a clear vision of Santorini and stayed true to it by painting the stairs white. It was the right call.

Stairway to heaven

A modern take on a Santorini kitchen. We took a minimalist approach in this kitchen by using discreet cabinet fronts with no handles and fully integrated appliances. We drew attention to the island bench (with its amazing mitred waterfall edge), climbing Caesarstone splashback (with drop-down rangehood) and hanging greenery.

Max out millimetres

Benchtops and cabinetry are typically 600 mm deep, however, you may need to increase this along your main kitchen wall to at least 700 mm in order to accommodate your cooktop. And go even deeper if necessary, to make sure your fridge doesn't stick out (eek!). Remember to allow at least 200 mm clearance on either side of your cooktop so you can turn your saucepan handles outwards (basically, the more millimetres, the merrier).

OUR MOST DISCREET CABINETS

The handles used in Lana's kitchen are discreet finger-pulls. They're a popular choice because they look chic and clean, and they let the cabinetry dominate the aesthetic. These finger-pulls are easy to clean (no fiddly handles to wipe around), but you will have to clean them regularly as the rebated channel can collect dust and food crumbs.

THE RIGHT BENCHTOP CAN MAKE OR BREAK YOUR KITCHEN

We spend a lot of time thinking about benchtops when designing kitchens because there are so many options to choose from. Our favourite material is Caesarstone, which is also referred to as quartz. It's man-made and has been augmented to have superpowers that real marble can't emulate. Specifically, engineered stone is stronger and harder, making it more scratch-resistant and chip-resistant. Its impenetrable surface also makes it much more stain-resistant and scorch-resistant. #wonderwoman It's not entirely infallible though – it can chip if you get unlucky and drop something on one of the edges, but that can usually be repaired.

DESIGN FOR EVERYDAY LIFE

You might love to entertain, but please don't sacrifice what you would prefer to live with every day for the sake of what looks nicer when visitors pop by once a month. For example, do you put the kitchen sink on the back bench, out of full view of visitors so things look tidy when you have a dinner party, or do you put it smack bang in the middle of the kitchen island, so you can face everyone while you work in the kitchen and watch the TV when washing up? We think you should choose the option that suits your everyday lifestyle best. Lana did!

Lana's compromises

STYLE VS. FUNCTION

Renovating is often about compromise but you should still be able to create a kitchen that looks good AND works well. Just be warned that at every turn, you may have to make decisions that feel like a trade-off. Here are a few examples of decisions Lana had to make when designing her kitchen.

01

Not locating the oven at eye level (a popular location these days) because it would have ruined the white, streamlined look she wanted.

02

Going without handles on the integrated fridge (even though handles would have made it easier to open) because, again, it would have interrupted the overall aesthetic.

03

Forgoing additional storage, with no overhead cabinetry above the cooktop, because she wanted the splashback to run up to the ceiling.

04

Locating the sink on the island bench rather than on the back bench because she wanted to be able to look out onto the rest of the room while standing at the sink, even though this meant dishes drying on the draining board would be more visible.

LAYER UP YOUR LOUNGE ROOMS

When it comes to designing lounge rooms, we always start by choosing the biggest furniture items first and then moving on to all the soft stuff (i.e. cushions, pillows, poufs, throws and rugs). We use these soft elements to add layers to a room and finish off the colour palette. For Lana's main family lounge room, which is next to the kitchen, we kept the sofa pale and neutral, and the cushions more muted. The rug gave us our pop of colour. In her secondary living area (above), we did the inverse. A teal couch became the statement piece so we opted for a neutral rug and ottoman to tone things down and allow the couch to remain the hero of the room.

THE GREENER, THE BETTER!

Greenery is an absolute must-have in the homes we design. We are yet to come across a space that wouldn't benefit from a plant of some description. They add colour, freshness and that feeling that 'THIS IS HOME!' In Lana's white-on-white home, hanging plants above the island and by the window add pops of brightness. P.S. Go faux! The hanging plant you see here is fake, so it always looks the goods!

66

Off-centre art

It's best to hang artwork at eye level but that doesn't mean it always has to be centred. Sometimes it's more interesting to position it off to one side, like we did here.

Light + view = the business

Fixed windows are an economical choice when you don't need airflow but still want lots of natural light and perhaps a view. We love boxing them out and creating a picture window with built-in bench seating.

GIVE YOURSELF A HOME OFFICE TO BE PROUD OF!

If you're one of the thousands of people who now work from home some or all of the time, forget about squeezing your office into a cramped hallway or under the stairs. Renovating your home is a golden opportunity to give yourself the best position in the house. For Lana, that meant claiming the light-filled room at the top of that showstopping staircase for her home office. It's large and airy with the best views. She figured if she was going to spend that much time working from home, why not enjoy it? Her home office is bright, beautiful and a space that makes her want to sit down and open her laptop. Creating this office was a total game changer for Lana, and it could be for you, too.

UPGRADE TO FAB FURNITURE

Forget the fluoro lights and swivel chairs, office decor need not be boring. This is your own office so you can make it ah-mazing! Choose a luxe rug and quilted chair, and don't be shy to add a gorgeous chandi above your desk. The better it looks, the more you'll love working in it. Check out Bon's home office on page 197 for more inspo.

A FEW MORE HOME (OFFICE) TRUTHS

- ♥ Depending on the climate you live in, having fresh air circulating through your office, feeding your lungs and brain, can be energising. Look around your space. Is there anything you can do to increase airflow?
- ♥ Work, by definition, isn't always fun, but that doesn't mean the place where it happens can't be beautiful. Statement pieces can add unexpected excitement to an office. If you fall in love with a fancy chandelier, who cares if it's not standard office furniture. Hang it loud and proud right over your desk. And you know what? It will make you happy every time you see it.

MOVE OVER 'BUTLER'S PANTRY', THERE'S A NEW SHERIFF IN TOWN

HELLO, BUTLER'S OFFICE!

Lana doesn't 'believe in' butler's pantries. To her mind, the babushka doll idea of a kitchen within a kitchen is flawed. If you have two kitchen spaces you can spend time in, why would you ever choose the smaller one? Lana thinks having a closed-off butler's kitchen defeats the whole purpose of open-plan living. (We can't really argue with her logic.)

Lana was never going to have a butler's pantry in her home. The space that would be a much-coveted butler's pantry in someone else's home became what she calls her 'butler's office' (that's right, she has two offices!). It's a smallish open-plan workspace (Lana's is about 4 square metres) located next to the kitchen, and connected to the other living spaces around it.

This butler's office was a real innovation for us – something Lana designed from scratch based on the needs of her family. It's not for everyone, but it definitely works in this kitchen thanks to the fact that it's cleverly concealed behind a half-wall and placed on a raised platform, which helps to separate and define the two zones.

The beauty of a butler's office is that it allows mums and dads to float between serving afternoon tea and closing a mega-deal via email, or pay some bills while waiting for a pot to boil. It's also a great place for kids to do their homework, especially if they're at an age where they need a little help with it or require some discreet supervision during screen time. It's getting harder to separate work and family life, so if this is an issue for you, maybe it's time to embrace it!

The butler's office

LANA'S BRAINCHILD

THINK ABOUT YOUR WINDOW SITUATION

Natural light is certainly the best and cheapest form of lighting. If you're thinking of adding new windows to your bathroom, make sure you know exactly what the view will be, and who might be able to see in. Sure, you can always choose frosted glass and shutters for privacy, but those won't help when you want to leave your window open. Having said that, casement-style windows in frosted glass can be opened on a tight angle, making it almost impossible for someone to see in.

AND DON'T MOVE THE WINDOW

Whenever possible, we say leave the existing window where it is and create your layout around it. Baths are perfect for squeezing in under windowsills.

ALL BATHS ARE NOT CREATED EQUAL

Back-to-wall baths are a bit of a hybrid between a freestanding style and a built-in. They look just like a freestanding bath, but they've been designed to be pushed up hard against the long-side wall and sealed. This is a fabulous way to get the freestanding look in a space-efficient manner, but without the hassle of soggy dust collecting behind the bath. Lana put a back-to-wall bath in her kids' bathroom and she reckons it looks even better than if it had been a regular freestanding bath.

Two in one!

Rail showers are height-adjustable, making them perfect for keeping your hair dry or showering little kids. Lana chose one with two showerheads in this bathroom so she could wash both kids at the same time. She's a true multitasker!

CREATE A MASTER SUITE ESCAPE

There are a few key elements that go into creating a master suite that really blows your hair back, and one of them is deciding on a statement piece. Regardless of which style of bedroom you're going for, most people want their bedroom to be a relaxing escape from the rest of world. And nothing says 'close your eyes, breathe in and relax' more than a beautiful ceiling fan. You wouldn't think it possible for a ceiling fan to be the star of the room, but we put these leaf-shaped fans in Lana and Bonnie's master suites and we've been inundated with 'OMG – THOSE FANS!' comments ever since.

CONSIDER YOUR BED FRAME

Your linen and cushion choice will ultimately create the style of your bed, but the bed frame plays an important role too. Our advice here is similar to the advice we give about choosing frames for artwork. The colour needs to complement the rest of the room, so if you opt for a timber frame, make sure it works with the colour of your floors – especially if they are also timber. We find black or wrought-iron frames less versatile than white or timber ones. If in doubt, it's hard to go wrong with a white bed frame, or even safer, an ensemble base (where there is no frame at all).

OPT FOR CARPET

There are so many price points and options when it comes to choosing carpet, you really can find something to match your style and budget. Lana put wool in her house because she wanted a natural fibre, and the large loop style felt beautiful underfoot. As with clothing, 100% wool carpets are a natural, premium, high-quality choice.

COMBINE FLOORING WISELY

If you're going to have different flooring throughout the house (say carpet in the bedrooms and floorboards everywhere else), make sure those two types of flooring look good together. Get samples of both, in different colours if you need to, and put them next to each other.

What lies beneath

Don't forget to budget for underlay when planning to use carpet. If you order a high-quality or sound-reducing underlay, this cost will sting if you're not expecting it.

DRESS YOUR ENSUITE TO IMPRESS

Designing a bathroom is kinda like choosing an outfit for a night on the town: you pick your favourite piece of clothing first, then build the rest of your outfit around that (sound familiar?). Same goes for bathrooms. Choose that 'wow' item first and then make everything else work in with it. In Lana's ensuite, the wow is unquestionably the amazing turquoise feature wall we created with the fish scale tiles. With this as the feature, everything else in the room had to be toned down.

IS A TILED FEATURE WALL RIGHT FOR YOU?

A tiled feature wall should provide a pop of colour or pattern, so we always recommend choosing the feature tile first, and then any other tiles you use in that space will have to work in around that. Keep the rest of the tiles in the bathroom muted – with either neutral colours like black, white or a marble-look. We usually only use two types of tile in a bathroom: one tile for the feature wall and then a neutral tile for the floor and remaining three walls. This really helps that feature wall pop, while the other three walls and floors visually merge into one. After deciding on turquoise fish scale tiles for her shower, Lana chose inexpensive 600 x 600 mm porcelain tiles for the floor to free up her budget for those pricier, but glorious, feature tiles. Putting your money into a small feature wall and then using basic tiles everywhere else is a smart way to divvy up your tile budget.

DON'T REINVENT THE (TILE) WHEEL

There are so many tiles to choose from, but that doesn't mean you should feel obliged to come up with a completely original tiling scheme on your own. If you have something very specific in mind that you want to try, go for it – but if you want more of a sure thing, look at what others have done and take your inspo from there. If you really love something, feel free to copy the tile and pattern exactly. There's no patent on tile patterns and you'll probably feel more at ease knowing that you are spending money on a scheme you've seen before and already love.

SHOW OFF YOUR BATHROOM'S BEST ANGLES

Bathroom doors are often left open to signal that the the room is vacant, right? With that in mind, make sure your bathroom's layout passes the 'walk-past test' – i.e. what can you (and your guests) see when walking past your bathroom (from any direction) and upon entering it? Ideally, you want to have the gorgeous stuff, like a feature wall, a statement bath or a vanity with mirror on show. Keep the toilet hidden. (Full disclosure: in some of our earlier renos we didn't manage to hide the toilet, but it is definitely always our aim.) In Lana's ensuite, much of her design was influenced by what could be seen when walking down the hallway towards the bathroom (which, incidentally, has no door). We also wanted to create a resort-style feel so we designed the layout to ensure one end of the beautiful bath and the trio of hanging greenery above were the only elements visible from the hall.

SHOWER SMARTS

Like many of us, Lana didn't want a door on her ensuite shower. If you opt not to have a door on your shower, you need to make sure your shower screen is long enough to prevent overspray and you'll also need a strong 'fall' on the floor to keep the water flowing towards the drain. We spent ages designing the walk-in shower for Lana's ensuite and the measurements worked out perfectly. The glass pane is 1000 mm long, leaving an opening of 640 mm.

We prefer using frameless glass for showers whenever possible.

THIS GLASS IS 'CHANNEL-SET', MEANING NO HINGES NECESSARY.

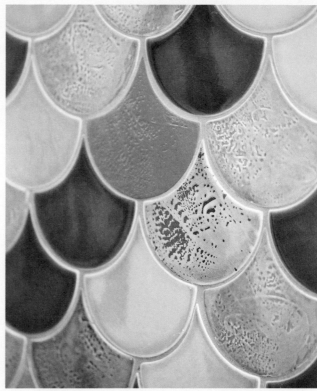

TILING TIPS

01

Use tiles from the same batch – this is really important as different batches can have noticeably different colours.

02

Order 10–15% extra tiles to ensure you have enough to cover off-cuts and damaged tiles.

03

Don't start tiling until you've checked you have enough tiles to complete the area.

04

Check all the tiles for shade variations before your tiler starts to lay them.

05

Tell your tiler you expect him not to lay any tiles that aren't the right colour or shade.

06

Store any leftover tiles in a safe place in case you ever need to replace one or two. This will guarantee they match.

07

Decide early if you want to have a cornice in your bathroom or a square set ceiling. This will impact how your tiler sets out the tiles and also how they are finished at the top.

08

Remember that you need to make all these decisions well before your reno begins to ensure your tiler can accurately quote the job and that you can get the amount of tiles you want on site by the date your tiler needs to start. #theearlybirdgetsthetile

FISH SCALE TILES: UP OR DOWN?

We've laid these both ways. For an art deco look, lay them curve up; for the mermaid look (like we went for here), lay them curve down.

WALL-MOUNTED TAPS

Wall-mounted taps provide more space behind the basin for standing toiletries, however, they will be more difficult to repair as you may need to open up the wall. Also take note that if those pipes are housed in a wall, you won't be able to have a cavity-sliding door on that same wall. Before you buy any tapware, make sure the spout will extend far enough over your basin – ideally, it should sit above the drain hole. This might sound obvious, but you'd be surprised how often spouts fall short. For this reason, it's best to choose your basin and tapware together.

SHOW YOUR LAUNDRY SOME LOVE

A laundry is a discreet zone where we like to have a bit of fun and try something different. Bonnie took this philosophy to a whole new level in her home (check out page 206 and brace yourself for pure amazingness!). Lana's laundry is a great example of doing something different that still fits with the overall vision for her home. She chose completely different tiles to the bathrooms, but they were gorgeous beachy pebbles that still ticked the box of her theme, Santorini in Sydney. To save some coin, don't tile all the walls. A lick of paint will do. Lana chose a pale blue/green tint to bring the Mediterranean Sea to her pebbled beach.

AIR IT OUT!

Of all the rooms in the house, the laundry probably needs ventilation the most. Good airflow will help keep it free from dreaded moisture and mould. An external window or door works best – especially a window that can be locked open while you are out. If you have a door but no window, consider a glass louvre door. It's just like a louvre window inserted into a door frame – perfect for keeping that air flowing. If your laundry doesn't have access to fresh air (as many don't), an exhaust fan is a must. If you have a Euro-style laundry, put the fan in the ceiling of the cupboard. In fact, it's a good idea to install an exhaust in every laundry so you can use it on those cold days when you don't want to open the laundry to the outside. Having said that, 'condensing dryers' dramatically reduce the moisture in a laundry – if your ventilation options are limited, this might be a good choice.

REDUCE THE NOISE FACTOR

Even though it's good to keep your laundry near the action, try to avoid locating it right next door to a bedroom or even a lounge room. No matter which washing machine you buy, it will still make some noise, especially when it's spinning. If you're constructing a new laundry room, you can choose building materials (like sound-reducing insulation and plasterboard) that will limit the noise coming from inside your laundry. A solid core door will also help keep the noise down.

Don't bend, sit!

A little stool in the laundry can make loading and unloading your front-loader so much easier. And it can look mighty cute too!

Lana went for these *amazing* pebble-like tiles in her laundry, but if your laundry is going to double as a *mud room*, large format tiles would be a better choice, as they're easier to clean and have fewer grout lines.

Lana

"When it came to designing the bedrooms for my kids, I wanted to stay away from the bright colours and materials used for a lot of 'kiddie' furniture. I love the look of timber and rattan, and wanted to use things like woven baskets that could be functional, but also a bit unexpected in a child's room. This style will be able to grow with them."

ENCOURAGE SOME DESK TIME

Setting up a clean and fun desk for your child to use can be a great way to get them into the groove of doing arts and crafts, and later the inevitable … homework!

Bargain buy!

These second-hand doors
were $40 each.

Double doona

LAYER THOSE LITTLE LINENS

Just because they're kids doesn't mean a basic sheet set will do. Splurge on extra pillows, throws and even a second doona to add layers of softness and extra 'fluff'. Style one as you would a normal doona (folded out) then place the second doona folded in half at the base of the bed. Don't overdo the pops of colour or the patterns – when it comes to making a statement, less is more. We went for some pin-tucks and cute details here – making it girly, but still sweet and definitely not childish. There's plenty of texture, and a bit of 'gritty pretty' thanks to the rattan and timber details. A few pops of gold and pink balanced things out nicely and made it really special.

SHELVES SHOULDN'T BE BORING!

You can pick up fun floating shelves from specialist boutiques to display colourful items or pictures that are personal to your child. You can also buy see-through bookshelves that can be mounted low on the walls, at kiddie level. These eliminate the need for a standing bookcase and also mean the book covers are on display, which adds colour and fun to the room in a way that's easily updated.

BE CLEVER ABOUT STORAGE

When we design bedrooms, we try to avoid taking up floor space with furniture – that means we don't go for chests of drawers or freestanding wardrobes. Instead, we look for every opportunity to create 'out of sight' storage, whether that's built-in wardrobes, walk-in dressing rooms or (one of our favourites) under-bed storage. There are loads of beds with pull-out drawers around now, and these drawers often offer MORE storage than a chest of drawers. It's a great place to stash linens, pyjamas, bath towels and bedding without crowding the room.

Most builders will include standard **skirting, architrave and cornice profiles** in their quotes. If you upgrade to a more decorative shape or profile, be aware you'll also be upgrading in price. In your Forever Home this may be worth it, but if you're looking to save money, this can be a good place to be economical.

BEFORE

LANDSCAPING, AKA THE FORGOTTEN CHILD

A great garden has the ability to make your house feel like a home you never want to leave. But even so, it's easy to focus attention inside and forget about the backyard. When we first started renovating houses, we were totally guilty of this. We didn't plan properly and under-budgeted in this area. But we learned our lesson quickly – there's nothing worse than a beautifully renovated home with a scrappy-looking garden.

BUY BI-FOLD, IF YOU CAN

Bi-fold doors are definitely the 'crème de la crème' of doors, especially for large openings as they stack at one end without blocking views or access. We re-used Lana's original blue bi-folds to 'unzip' the back of her house and simply painted them white. The large opening seamlessly connects the inside and out. The best thing about bi-folds is that they pretty much suit any style of house. The downside (apart from the 'ain't cheap' factor) is that when closed, they interrupt your view more than other doors, like large sliders, which have less framework. It comes down to deciding between the vista when open or the vista when closed. It's also important to discuss with your builder what finished height the bi-fold floor track will sit at. The best tracks are recessed into the floor so they end up flush, meaning there's nothing to step over when walking from inside to out.

Already got a gorgeous garden?

If the answer is yes, talk to your builder about how to best protect it, what damage might occur and who is responsible for repairing any damage. At the very least, your turf will likely be destroyed, so plan for that.

AFTER

Hello, holiday vibes!

AHHH, FEEL THAT INDOOR/ OUTDOOR FLOW

A great trick when trying to make an outside space feel like a seamless continuation of the inside is to use the same ceiling lining. So, for example, if you have a panelled ceiling with exposed rafters inside, continue those same panels and rafters outside. Here, we continued Lana's white panelled ceilings right out over her alfresco area, giving her family a place to relax and enjoy. – rain or shine.

CLASSING UP THE SERVERY

Don't you just love having a bar-height place to perch in an alfresco area? It's even better when the servery runs seamlessly from inside to out. In fact, we've included an inside/outside servery in almost every house we've done, so it would've been criminal not to put one in Lana's home! Ideally, the depth of the servery should be a minimum of 500 mm inside plus 300 mm outside (for a total of 800 mm when the window is open). Lana went with these measurements for hers. However, if space is limited, you can get away with a 300 mm depth on the inside. Lana also chose to run a single slab of Caesarstone from inside the kitchen to outside – when the window is open, it becomes an intimate eight-seater dining table (which we've put to the test many times with great success).

SIZE MATTERS (WITH FURNITURE)

When it comes to outdoor furniture, bigger is NOT better. You need to be able to move around the furniture and easily get in and out of the table or lounge setting. Lana's deck is a good example of how tight you can go. Although it's a relatively long deck (10 metres), it's quite skinny (3.2 metres) so it provided a great challenge for us when it came to how much furniture we could squeeze in.

GOTTA HAVE THAT HANDRAIL!

Take note that if your alfresco area is higher than 1 metre off the ground, most building codes state that you need to have a handrail/balustrade. Not only will this prevent your friends and family from taking a tumble, it can also impact the look and feel of your outdoor space. Frameless glass is a great option if you want to maintain an unobstructed view – especially if you'll be seated at lounge level and looking through, rather than over, the balustrade. Glass also provides the clearest view for watching kids in the pool. A cheaper option is a timber balustrade (which your carpenter or landscaper can build and paint) but this might block your view and/or not suit the look of your house. Having said that, white balustrades usually look amazing (see page 43).

GAS STRUT G.L.O.R.Y

Gas-strut windows are the bee's knees. In fact, you could say they've become a bit of a trademark of a Three Birds reno! Here's why we think gas-strut windows are so great:

01

They offer an unobstructed view when closed, versus bi-folds, which have framework around each little window leaf.

02

They are so easy to open. Nudge the window and it opens up like it's motorised. But take note, if you make the window too tall, you might need a stool (or a tall friend) to help you close it.

03

They are such a space saver compared to bi-folds, which stack up to one side, taking up valuable servery space.

04

When open, they can act as an awning and provide cover from rain.

05

Their design is inherently cool, so they bring a relaxed beachy vibe to the space.

06

They are a bit cheaper than bi-folds.

07

Umm, they just look so damn fine! #obsessed

Lana's bougainvillea

This gorgeous bougs had been growing at Lana's for years, and it became the key to her Santorini in Sydney vision. Everyone who stepped on site (including a poor postie!) was told it had to be protected at all costs. It's now happily climbing those white walls, and if it doesn't say Santorini, we don't know what does.

BEFORE

USE IT OR LOSE IT

Please don't forget to pay attention to all four sides of your home when dreaming up your reno. You want to create a plan that works for the front, the back and the sides of your home. One of the biggest transformations at Lana's house happened when the side of her home went from being nothing more than an ugly thoroughfare to an entertainer's delight. This transformation involved lots of hardscaping (meaning decks, walls and paving) but it made a BIG difference.

WE LOVE A BUILT-IN BENCH SEAT

We installed the ultimate bench seat on this side deck. It's about 6 metres long and could probably seat 20 people, if needed. It helps to create that 'outdoor room' vibe and provide loads of practical seating options. Whether you use a bench seat to optimise a corner space, or to provide seating along one side of a dining table, bench seats are an #alfrescowin. They're practical and pretty, not to mention pretty cheap to build. When designing your alfresco area, make sure you look around and ask yourself, 'Where could I build a sneaky little bench seat?' Get your carpenter to knock one up for you, add a splash of paint and voila!

AFTER

SPLASH OUT

The crowning glory of Lana's garden is her pool. It's the finishing touch that gives her home that 'on holiday every day' vibe she was dreaming of at the start of the renovation. But, as we discovered, building a pool isn't as straightforward as you might think. As with everything else in the world of renovation, there's a lot to learn and research. Lana started with the look she was after. Once you know that, you are ready to embark on the next big decision – fibreglass or concrete? True story, Lana never knew the difference between them until she started getting quotes. Fibreglass and concrete are both great options. You just need to work out which one best meets your needs. (Bonnie went with concrete for her pool, so head to page 224 to find out why that was the best option for her.)

THE MANY PROS OF FIBREGLASS POOLS

01

Cheaper They usually cost around 20% less than a concrete pool to build and install, and ongoing costs are lower due to these pools requiring less maintenance, fewer chemicals and energy.

02

Faster Installation takes only 3 weeks vs. 3 months for a concrete pool. In fact, we've heard they can be installed in 3 days (surely not?)!

03

Gentler The non-abrasive surface is softer on your feet (no torn-up tootsies) and fibreglass is not as rock-hard as concrete if your kids accidentally hit the bottom.

04

Warmer Fibreglass acts as a natural insulator so it holds in the heat for longer.

05

Cleaner The gel-coating is smooth and non-porous, which makes it easier to clean.

06

Greener Less cleaning + less chemicals + less energy consumption = a smaller carbon footprint.

07

Stronger It's hard to believe anything is stronger than concrete but fibreglass is very durable and can even withstand movements in the earth better than concrete.

Blue hues

Before locking in your colour, ask your pool company if you can visit some of the pools they've installed. Nothing beats eyeballing the real thing before making your final decision.

TAKE YOUR PRETTY TIME CHOOSING YOUR POOL COLOUR

We can guarantee you will LOOK at your pool more often than you swim in it, so don't rush the CRUCIAL decision of choosing your pool colour. For many people, it's their shortcut to a 'water view', so you should love the colour from afar as much as you do when immersed in it.

DON'T FORGET ABOUT DECKING

We are constantly asked what type of timber Lana used for her pool deck (opposite) and how she achieved that look. She wanted a pale grey deck so she did a huge amount of research on how to achieve that natural, silvered look. Lana found a product called Cutek CD-50 Oil that protects the timber while allowing it to silver naturally (though you could also add colour to it if you wanted a stained look). The timber has silvered beautifully and she could not be happier with it.

LIMITATIONS OF FIBREGLASS

The biggest drawback with fibreglass pools is that there are limitations when it comes to design and colour. They are pre-made and can only be bought 'off the rack', whereas a concrete pool can be custom-made just for you. Having said that, there is a huge range to choose from, and many modern fibreglass pools come with swim-outs and lounge areas built into the pool shell so they're worth checking out. These pools need to be transported by road so their width is limited to around 4.2 metres (this should be wide enough for most backyards). The other thing to keep in mind is that a crane is usually needed to lift the pool shell off the truck and into your backyard. This can sometimes be tricky but it is something that will be managed by the pool installers.

The luxe entertainer

Our *upside-down* house

The houses we like to buy and renovate have a great footprint that don't require a major extension, like a second storey, to add value. By opening up the floorplan, cosmetically changing the outside (say, by spraying the brick and adding a new timber balustrade) and adding a modern alfresco space in the backyard, they can be quickly transformed into dream family homes.

But many older two- and three-storey houses are built on sloping blocks, and specifically on blocks that slope downward from the street towards the back fence. In these houses, the kitchen is often on the middle or upper level, as you enter the house at street level. Usually, this means the lowest level becomes a rumpus room, garage, 'man cave' or separate living quarters. Know any houses like that?

The limitation with this design is that the bottom level is actually the one that flows out onto the backyard. Ideally, that's where you want your living spaces in order for your family to be able to enjoy that direct connection with the alfresco area, whether that's a deck or a paved section. This area in turn should (hopefully) connect with some grass and, space-permitting, perhaps even a pool. This layout is especially important if you want to keep an eye on the kids when they're playing outside. By flipping this house's layout on its head and bringing more natural light into the inside spaces, we were able to turn it into a modern home that functions so well for real family life.

Holy reno inspo!

BEFORE

AFTER

BEFORE

THE ORIGINAL STAIRCASE WAS A PROBLEM ...

It was a funnel. A coat of paint wasn't going to fix this problem – we knew we needed to perform some serious stairway surgery. We removed a wall and the floor to create a huge void next to the stairwell, completely transforming this narrow space from funnel to fabulous and flooding the areas downstairs with natural light. This exact staircase and void was the inspiration behind the staircase/void combo we later designed for Lana's Forever Home (page 60). She was so blown away by how open and airy this house felt after we made these changes that she decided she needed more of that in her life.

THE PREVIOUSLY DARK, SKINNY RUMPUS ROOM WAS TRANSFORMED

In its place was a light and airy entertainer's kitchen, a beautiful dining area and a lounge that opened right up to the outdoor area. The challenge was making the kitchen look as big as possible, so of course we used lots of white through this whole space. We also installed multiple French doors along the exterior wall to let in even more natural light.

Lana's advice to anyone considering a staircase/void combo is *just do it!*

AFTER

Stone cold stunner

One of the best decisions we made in this kitchen was running the Calacatta engineered stone benchtop up the wall as a luxe splashback.

BLINGBLING

PENDANT PERFECTION

If you're going to have an island in your kitchen (and we think you should!), the number of pendants you need depends on the size of your island and the size of the pendant lights (both can vary greatly). We've used pendant lights that are just 20 cm wide and, at the other end of the spectrum, we've also installed a chandelier 1.4 metres wide in Bonnie's kitchen (check out page 201)! Looking back at our kitchen renos, we've never hung more than two pendants over our island benches. So, here is our advice:

- For an island 1500–1800 mm long, go for two average-sized pendant lights (under 40 cm in diameter) centred over the island.
- For an island 1800–3000 mm long, two average-sized pendant lights hung off-centre over the island look great. So, in this instance you would space them out as if there were going to be three lights, but only install two.
- For an island over 3000 mm long you can definitely consider three average-sized pendants or supersize them and just use two.

MATT OR GLOSSY CABINETRY?

Neither! We prefer a satin finish that sits somewhere in between. Gloss can be quite reflective and shows imperfections, water drips, scratches and fingerprints. At the other end of the spectrum, matt cabinetry can feel a bit flat and dull. It also shows fingerprints and can be hard to clean. Then there's satin – with a low-sheen finish, it's super-smooth to touch, non-reflective and doesn't show fingerprints. It's also easy-peasy to wipe clean. What's not to love?

KITCHEN HARDWARE

We used tiny black knobs from IKEA on these cabinets, which look great and are perfect for these lightweight drawers. If you're planning to fill them with heavy items, like plates or pots, you might need to go for larger knobs.

FLIP TIP

Your best bet is to choose engineered stone for most mid- to high-end property flips. #cantgowrong And for homes at the lower end of the market or investment properties, laminate might be a smarter choice. If you do go with laminate, don't choose a style that tries to mimic marble or timber – a plain colour is less likely to draw attention to the 'fake factor'. If you're still unsure which way to go, ask your local real estate agent or jump online to see what type of benchtops are in the homes being sold in that suburb.

Budget buy alert!

We bought these cute-as-a-button black
knobs for just a few bucks from IKEA!

LET'S GET ILLUMINATED

Great lighting really can make a big difference to how your home feels so please do not under-budget or under-plan in this area. You'll thank us later! Nobody wants to live with sub-optimal lighting or look at a pendant hanging in the wrong spot every day. If you're tackling a whole home reno or a new build, you need to get your lighting plan locked in as soon as the framing goes up because your electrician ('sparky') will need to 'rough in' all the necessary wiring before the wall linings go on. There are three types of lighting you need to plan for, and to make it easy to remember, each one just happens to have it's very own Three Birds spirit animal ...

Bonnie

Ambient lighting

This is the Bonnie of the lighting world — the overall light source for a room and the one that creates atmosphere. This family of lighting includes downlights, pendants, chandeliers, wall sconces and floor lamps. Yes, we know that downlights aren't that sexy, but ignore them at your peril. In fact, we'll go as far as saying that failing to appreciate the importance of ambient lighting can actually MAKE OR BREAK the feel of your house. We like to mix things up by using a combo of downlights, sconces and pendants to light the ceilings and walls. We also love using floor lamps because they reflect light up to the ceiling, giving off a lovely soft glow that works really well in living areas. The key is to always go for warm white (rather than cool white) globes.

Erin

Task lighting

This lighting is for specific tasks, such as chopping food in the kitchen, reading in a bedroom or working in a home office. Like Erin, task lighting gets down to the business of doing business. By being very clear about what you want to achieve in each space, you'll be able to light it accordingly. This may mean installing a wall sconce in a reading nook, placing soft lighting at face level around a bathroom mirror or placing small lights in cupboards or wardrobes so you aren't hunting around for things in the dark.

Lana

Accent lighting

Like Lana, this is where the drama comes in! Accent lighting is used to highlight things that you want to draw attention to. This might mean putting spotlights above a piece of art, or lighting in a cabinet to illuminate the decorative objects on display. We haven't used that much accent lighting in the past, mainly because our first five renos were flip properties with tight budgets, so accent lighting seemed like a luxury we couldn't afford. However, if you're renovating your Forever Home, it's definitely worth considering. This type of lighting can be perfect in a hallway where you're likely to hang art that will benefit from being lit for extra drama. For The River Shack reno, we used an outdoor light inside to illuminate a picture window (see page 172).

'Just looks hot' lighting

OK, there is one other type of lighting we have not discussed and it is NOT widely written about. It's what Bon likes to call 'Just looks hot' lighting! Occasionally, we install a light for no reason other than it looks amazing, on or off. We put these types of lights in every house and think of them more as works of art than functional lights.

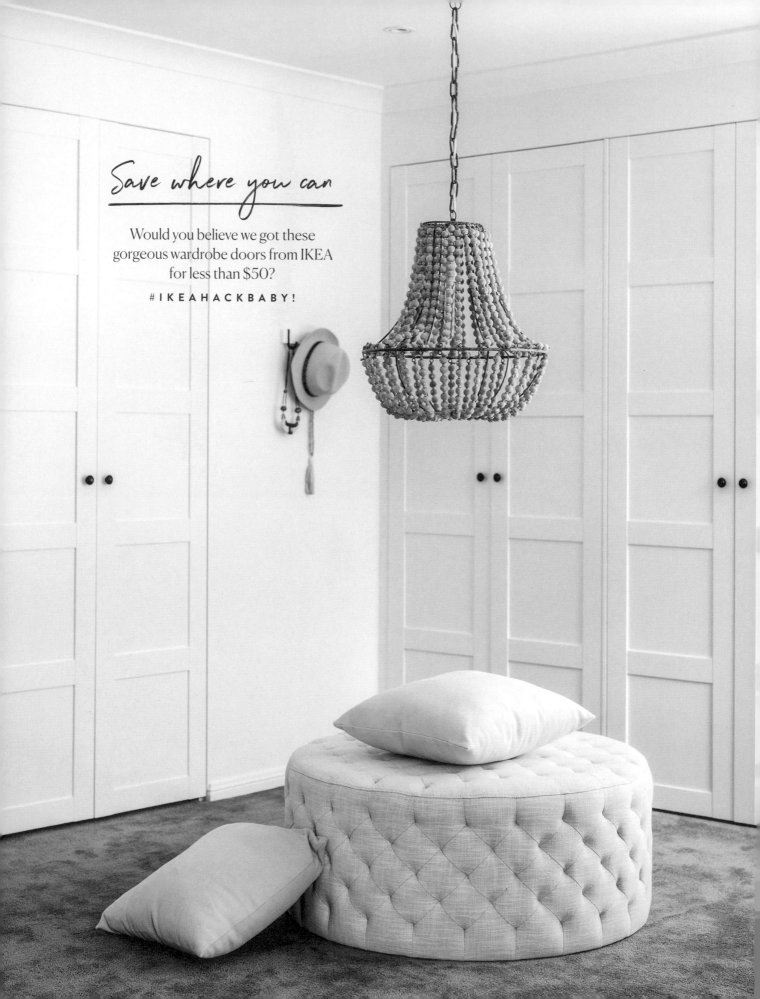

Save where you can

Would you believe we got these
gorgeous wardrobe doors from IKEA
for less than $50?

#IKEAHACKBABY!

Stop tiling here to
save money

Hey, savvy spender!

White subway tiles are a great go-to
when you're on a tight budget.

GO LUXE ON THE FLOOR

If you've decided a feature wall isn't for you, you can still introduce a little luxury and interest by choosing a slightly more expensive floor tile. Most bathrooms have less floor space than wall space, so you won't need to spend as much to make a feature of your floor while keeping the walls basic and affordable. The hexagonal marble tiles we used in this reno take this simple white bathroom up a few levels by adding a touch of drama and impact.

HIDE THE TOILET (IF YOU CAN)

Try to avoid placing the toilet in clear view of the door. This is harder than it sounds. This picture was taken from the doorway, and this is the ideal view – the beautiful bath is on display and the toilet is hidden to the right.

SHOULD YOU MOVE THE SERVICES?

There's no arguing that it's cheaper to keep the plumbing services (i.e. all the pipes and drains) where they already are, but the compromise on enjoyment of that space is often too great for us; it's like rearranging the deck chairs on the Titanic – what's the point? If you're going to bother with the mess, dust and money of a bathroom reno, make it count by getting the layout right. A flash new toilet won't be as enjoyable if the door hits it every time someone walks in.

RESIST THE URGE TO TILE FLOOR TO CEILING

Save on materials and labour in bathrooms by tiling only 1.2 metres up from the floor (except for the shower recess, of course) and then paint the rest of the walls. That's what we did here. It looks great, plus it cut our tiling bill in half and gave the bathroom a softer feel, with fewer hard shiny surfaces.

DON'T FORGET THE NICHE

You know that cut-out in your shower wall where you store shampoo and body wash? Well, if you don't communicate where you want it and how big it should be early on, you'll find the shower wall has been 'sheeted' and waterproofed and you've missed your opportunity for a niche.

FLIP TIP

Ditch the built-in bath: This is a real win-win as far as cost and style are concerned. Freestanding baths are not only cheaper to install than built-ins (requiring less framework, waterproofing and tiling), they also look so damn sexy!

107

Concrete pavers laid in a 'French lay' pattern

EASY AND ELEGANT

WINDOWS AND DOORS GALORE

The openings we added to the back of this house made all the difference to the light and indoor/outdoor flow of the house. If we could unzip the back of every house and have the whole thing open, completely unobstructed, we would! The cost and practicalities involved are often significant but that doesn't mean you can't put in as many openings as humanly (or structurally) possible, like we did with these French doors. Chat with your structural engineer to find out what's possible, and within budget. Have this conversation very early on – before submitting your plans to council.

PAVERS TO THE RESCUE

Because decks require some height (at least 5 cm) to lift them off the ground and provide necessary ventilation, you may have to dig down to create that space or endure a little step-up onto your deck (not a good look when flush floor heights are key to creating that seamless transition from inside to out). This is where pavers can be a great solution. We'd intended to build a huge deck running the width of this house, but when we got the quotes back from a few landscapers, we moved to Plan B – building a small deck at one end and paving the rest. Paving is usually cheaper than decking, and we chose affordable concrete pavers that looked like limestone. They were laid in a 'French lay' pattern and the result was stunning. By using these two materials we created two distinct zones in that backyard; the decking provided a lounge zone, and the paving was perfect for dining.

CONVERTIBLE FIRE PIT

Fire pits are growing in popularity. They bring people together in a 'round the camp fire' kind of way and truly allow you to enjoy your outdoor space all year round. But you'll probably want to use that space for something else come spring and summer, so versatility is the name of the game. An alfresco space that can be changed up is #renogold. We constructed a space for this fire pit and gave it its own drainage, wrap-around seating and herringbone pavers. In summer, simply replace the fire pit with a coffee table and a large shade umbrella and you've got a sunken sun lounge!

FRENCH DOORS ARE AFFORDABLE

We love using these beauties, which you should be able to pick up from your local hardware store without breaking the bank. Once they're painted white, they make all our alfresco areas – even our low-budget ones – feel special. You'll need to buy door handles and some flush bolts separately, but that's the same with all doors. Your builder or carpenter should have no issues installing these doors quickly.

CREATE AN OUTDOOR ROOM

A strategically placed privacy screen that connects to a pergola or overhead covering can create the feeling of an outdoor room. They need only be about 1.6 to 1.8 metres high and you can buy pre-fabricated screens (like we used here), or go for a more solid structure by using fibre-cement planks, which we did in The New Classic (see page 128).

GREENERY IS A MUST

Nothing says sit down and relax like beautiful greenery, and the pot is often as important as the plant. Bigger is usually better when it comes to pots; a big plant bursting at the seams in a crummy little pot is a sad sight to behold. Give your greens room to grow!

FLIP TIP

We happen to think that sprayed bricks look great. So much so that this is one of our favourite tricks for a total transformation, especially on a budget. Not only does it cost a lot less than rendering or cladding, it can also be done so fast (like in a weekend) and in any colour under the sun! And don't think of it as a compromise on looks; one of our sprayed-brick properties (Hamptons in the hills) even made the front cover of a glossy magazine!

Easy extension

Paint the screen the same colour as the house to create a seamless continuation.

The new classic

Business up *front,* *party* at the back

With most of our flip properties, the big opportunity lies at the back of the house rather than the front – this house was no exception. It had all the trappings of a typical suburban home and a decent size footprint, but it had pokey little rooms, a tiny kitchen, no indoor/outdoor flow, an external laundry where you'd want the kitchen to be, no real alfresco area for entertaining and last, but not least, a rickety old Hills Hoist baring its soul in the heart of the backyard.

For us, the solution was simple. First up, we absorbed the external laundry into the footprint of a new kitchen to connect it directly to the outside with two new gas-strut windows and a wrap-around breakfast bar. #nobrainer! Next, we built a new deck off the existing concrete porch and ran it the full length of the house. With some fresh paint, privacy screening and an open pergola to create the feeling of an outdoor room, Bob's your uncle, it's a whole new world out there!

In case you're wondering why we removed the upstairs balcony, let us explain. It was broken and required rebuilding. #costly Plus, the view wasn't exactly spectacular (it looked straight into the neighbour's house). We also couldn't build an ensuite while it remained, so what might seem like an odd decision was actually an easy one for us on the day. And here's a tip: there are so many tough decisions when renovating that when an easy one comes along, you take it!

BEFORE

AFTER

Privacy please

We love open plan, but internal doors like these give you the option for privacy from time to time.

#SERENITYNOW

LOVELY LAMINATE

We used laminate flooring throughout this house. It simulates the look and feel of timber, but there's actually no timber used at all. It's made from compressed wood composite, cork, melamine and other materials. It looks like timber because of the photographic layer used on its surface, which is protected underneath a clear 'wear' layer. Laminate planks are basically a picture of wood, but not real wood. It's a great affordable alternative to the real thing.

TAPAS, ANYONE? #YESWAYJOSÉ

Even in our smaller homes, we like to create moments of indulgence and luxury. In this modest four-bedroom house, we created what Lana calls 'the tapas lounge' (seriously, that got printed in the real estate brochure!). It's a place for adults to host pre-dinner drinks, maybe some tapas, or even enjoy a quiet nightcap before bed. Whatever your flavour, this room has you covered.

Magic floors

Want a bigger house but can't afford an extension? Choose light-coloured flooring instead of dark – it makes the house look larger.

**Hanging pendant
lights over your table?**
Don't fall into the trap of hanging
them too high. Remember, you and
your guests or family will be seated, so the
pendants can hang lower than you might
think. These ones are just 500 mm
above the table, and they are the
perfect height.

MIX, DON'T MATCH

When buying a dining table, don't feel compelled to buy
a set of matching chairs. Sure, it can look nice and we've
done it before, but we also like to mix things up sometimes.
In this dining room, we used three different types of chairs
and it's those chairs that make the room so interesting.
P.S. We upcycled those two bamboo chairs at the back with
a can of spray paint and new upholstery. And how good do
they look?

PENDANTS DON'T NEED TO
BE PRICEY

In fact, you can pick up some gorgeous pendants at your
local hardware store for less than $100. Most shops will
allow you to return the pendants for a full refund, so it's
worth taking home a few options and holding them up.
#trybeforeyoubuy

RESTYLE THAT LOUNGE

Whether you're planning to do a small reno or a large one, we bet our budget that you'll want to style your lounge room differently. The kitchen may be the heart of the home, but the lounge room comes a close second. It's where the whole family comes together, so creating a comfortable and stylish lounge room that flows is a must. The good news is that this doesn't have to be a daunting or expensive task (see page 172 for some of our top tips).

CREATING BALANCE ISN'T NECESSARILY ABOUT SYMMETRY

Symmetry, i.e. when elements in a room perfectly mirror each other (think matching bedside tables or identical armchairs on either side of a couch), is a pretty traditional way of creating balance in a room. Of course it works really well, but we often prefer asymmetrical styling, which mixes things up a bit more. For us, balance is about distributing the visual weight in a room, and though this can be done with symmetry, that sort of arrangement can sometimes feel a little too formal. Asymmetrical balance brings a sense of casual living to a room, which is why we love using it. In this lounge, we popped an occasional table on one side of the couch and a large plant on the other, and chose coffee tables in different sizes. Even the art is a little off-centre. Contrast and variety add visual interest to a room. Try a few options when it comes to styling and play with asymmetry to see if it suits the look you're going for.

ADD INTEREST WITH PLANTS

But before you get potting, make sure you do your research on which plants are best suited to your home, as things like room temperature and sunlight play a huge role in what lives and what ends up in the bin. Some plants will burn when placed next to a window with too much direct sunlight, while others will thrive. We love using tall plants like fiddle-leaf figs or strelitzias in the corner of a room, or by a front door to add height and interest, but then we opt for small succulents and trailing plants for bathrooms, kitchens and shelves.

Bonnie

"One of the things I find hardest when trying to explain how I work is articulating what goes on in my head and heart when designing a room. I believe in trusting your gut and trying things out. I never know for sure how a room is going to look until I'm in the space, working up a sweat and moving things around. So grab some friends to help you out and just go for it."

A CLUSTER OF COFFEE TABLES

We aren't huge fans of big heavy coffee tables in a lounge room — they tend to dominate the space a bit too much. Multiple tables nested together are a better option because they provide flexibility when you are entertaining and are so easy to move around.

BEFORE

AFTER

OPEN UP YOUR KITCHEN AND EVICT THE ORIGINAL LAUNDRY!

To state the obvious, your kitchen should not be in a room of its own, if possible. That was the preference decades ago, but not today. Open-plan living is all the rage and for good reason. Kitchens should open out to a dining and lounge room wherever possible. In many older homes, the laundry (often an external one) was built right in the spot where you'd probably like to put your new kitchen – close to the backyard! This was done to provide quick and easy access to the washing line. In this house, we addressed this challenge by removing a wall and absorbing the old external laundry into our new kitchen footprint. This created an awesome entertainer's kitchen that connects directly to the backyard. ALWAYS relocate the laundry if it's where you'd prefer the kitchen to be. Remember, your kitchen is priority #1.

GREY IS THE 'NEW NEUTRAL'

It's now widely accepted as a mainstream colour for exteriors and kitchens alike, and we think grey is a beautiful alternative to white. If you don't want white (perhaps you think it's too boring), but still want to play it safe, we recommend pale grey – we love Silkwort by Dulux. Just like white, grey offers the perfect neutral canvas for bringing in splashes of colour and warmth through your choice of accessories. If you're not confident about going all the way with a colour, you can limit it to under-bench cabinetry and the island and use white for all of the overhead cabinets. #twotonebaby

CREATING A NEW CLASSIC

If cabinetry is going to be the statement feature in your kitchen, the splashback needs to take a back seat, and vice versa. Makes sense, right? This custom-made kitchen is the same silky grey colour as the feature stairwell (see page 123). Since cabinetry was the star, we went for stone benchtops in muted tones with soft grey veins and classic white square tiles in a brick pattern with light grout for the splashback. Matt black tapware, pendant lights and handles ensure this kitchen feels modern despite the more traditional splashback and shaker doors – hence a new classic!

3 KITCHEN LAYOUT TIPS

01

Ideally, your kitchen should connect to the outdoor entertaining area. That area can be located at the front, back or side of your house, but the best kitchen position will be close to it, so try to put it there on your plans. If you don't have an outdoor entertaining area, think about where you could create one.

02

Most kitchens have at least one wall of floor-to-ceiling cabinetry, with no space for windows. Think carefully about which side of the room to put this wall and, if you can, choose the side that gets the LEAST amount of natural light. That way you'll be letting in the maximum amount of natural light when you build your kitchen.

03

Put the fridge in a convenient place (at one end of the room, perhaps) so people can grab drinks from it without having to walk right through the middle of the kitchen.

BEFORE

From sad and neglected to useful and fab

WE LOVE FINDING DEAD SPACE!

It provides a real opportunity to add value by creating something out of nothing. By 'dead space' we mean space you're not using – you know, that area you probably avert your eyes from due to the pang of embarrassment. These areas can often be transformed with relatively minimal effort and cost. Sometimes dead space can be really tiny, like this area we transformed under the stairs. We added a reading nook by building a bench seat with a reading lamp and we used ship-lap wall cladding to add texture and dimension. Light grey paint and a fresh white balustrade created a quiet, peaceful feeling that was softened further by using cushions and a faux fur throw. This became one of our favourite spots in the house. Take a look around your home. Are there any nooks, inside or outside, that you could bring to life?

AFTER

ONE-COLOUR MOOD

Tiles are the best way to create a feature in your bathroom. Not only are there so many tiles to choose from, but they can often be laid in different ways with a choice of grout colours to create any number of looks. The standout feature of this bathroom was always going to be these gorgeous sea-foam subways. It's the only colour used in this bathroom and it packs an awesome punch against the large-format marble wall tiles and darker herringbone floor.

GROUT IS OFTEN AN AFTERTHOUGHT

This is because many people don't realise they have a choice beyond the standard grout. What a missed opportunity! Spending just a little time choosing your grout colour can have a very dramatic effect on the look of your bathroom. If you want your tiles to 'pop' as individual pieces, choose a contrasting grout colour; if you want the tiles to blend together and look like one big piece, choose a colour that matches the tiles. We used white grout in this bathroom to make the brick pattern in these subway tiles more visible.

TALK 'FALL' WITH YOUR TILER

Your tiler will ensure the floor slopes towards the drains and meets the required building standards – this is called the 'fall'. This slope is imperceptible to the eye but is necessary to send any water that finds its way onto the floor towards the drain, rather than leave it to pool on your floor. What's this got to do with tiles? Glad you asked; you see, the size and shape of your tiles will impact how easy (or hard) it is for the tiler to create the right fall without having to cut into your tiles and create loads of unsightly diagonal joins. Our advice is to get a sample of your preferred tile, show it to your tiler and discuss how they plan to create the right fall with this type of tile. Ask specifically if they will need to make any cuts and how they can avoid creating any ugly cuts. You'll be glad you did. Sometimes, part of the solution will be to add a long strip drain, but this won't be cheap.

CAN YOU ACCEPT A SMALL STEP UP?

When renovating a bathroom, your builder will usually ask if you want to lower the existing bathroom floor so the end result is flush with the adjoining room's floor height. The alternative is accepting a small step up when you enter the bathroom. In a perfect world all floors would be flush, but if money is tight, a little step is a small price to pay to avoid the costs of lowering the floor for the sake of a flush finish. Just be careful not to stub your toe in the middle of the night. #ouch

HANG YOUR VANITY

A wall-hung vanity is suspended in the air, affixed to the wall with sturdy bolts. It can be installed by your plumber, builder or cabinet-maker. Wall-hung vanities are great for giving the illusion of a bigger bathroom because your floor space is visible underneath the vanity.

Planning vanity

If a wall-hung vanity is your preferred style, take note that it cannot be a last-minute decision. You need to plan for it in advance and communicate your intentions to your builder so they can put in the studwork behind the wall that the vanity will be attached to. Also, let your plumber know so they can rough in the pipes behind the wall to make them invisible.

Walk-in-robe behind this floating wall

A BIG BED ISN'T ALWAYS BETTER

Who doesn't love a king-size bed? They're luxurious, and if you've got heaps of space we definitely recommend one. If you're styling an average-sized bedroom, be realistic and consider how the room will function when all of the furniture is in place. The number of people that are willing to shove a huge bed into a tiny room always amazes us – it looks awful and kills the flow of the room completely. If space is tight, use a single bed. If you're working with a smaller master suite, opt for a queen rather than king bed … and consider that a double bed would make the room feel even bigger.

GENEROUS DRESSING SPACE IS A MUST IN A MASTER

We like to move beyond the standard walk-in-robe (WIR) or built-in concept and create more of a luxurious dressing space. Usually this involves a floating wall, like the one here.

BEDSIDE TABLES

We often mix and match bedside tables to add a bit of variety to a bedroom. When choosing a bedside table, consider how it's going to be used. Does it need to be big enough to fit a lamp, a cup of tea and a book, or will a tiny round table do the trick? These tables are classic clutter-collectors, so if the person using the table has a tendency to leave magazines, piles of mail, cold cups of tea and other non-stylish items piled next to their bed, opt for a small, simple table that offers minimal 'storage' opportunities.

DITCH THE BEDSIDE LAMPS

Sounds a bit harsh, we know (sorry!), but we're yet to find a bedroom that isn't improved by replacing bedside lamps with beautiful wall sconces or pendant lights. Both of these options are elevated, so they don't clutter up bedside tables. They also look beautiful and provide warm, intimate lighting.

Solo styles

In small bedrooms, we suggest you only have one bedside table.

BEFORE BUYING ART

✔ Ask yourself if you need more than one piece of art on that wall to achieve your desired look. Would a series of two or perhaps a cluster of small frames be better than one large piece? If you're not too confident, stick with a single piece of art as making a gallery wall can be a bit trickier.

✔ Before you push the green button on your artwork purchase, use masking tape to map out its exact size and the intended location on the wall. This is particularly helpful when trying to work out how to cluster a bunch of smaller prints.

FLIP TIP

If you're selling your house, it's important to get the size and location of the beds right because you want potential buyers to see B-I-G bedrooms. Downsize the bed wherever you can. (But this doesn't mean putting single beds in every room. Eek! #backpackerslodge)

MAXIMISING THE OUTSIDE SPACES

Without a doubt, one of the biggest (and best) transformations at this house took place at the back. We ripped down the second-floor balcony and focused our efforts on making the ground floor deck a dream space. We created different zones, putting two seating areas in, adding privacy screening to create that outdoor room feeling and a pergola for interest.

FAKE IT OUTSIDE

We've already mentioned that we are big advocates of faux plants indoors, but did you know you can fake it outside too? This faux palm was super easy to manage while this house was on the market ... it never needed watering. #flippingperfect

PERGOLA TO THE RESCUE

When we're faced with an unloved outdoor area, we have a special saying here at Three Birds: 'If in doubt, add a pergola!' Pergolas don't need to cover the full alfresco area – they look fab when used in only part of the space as a design feature and can also signal a change in alfresco zones. Technically, pergolas are supposed to have an open framework, but you can add a polycarbonate roof for rain cover (like Bon did at her house on page 220) or perhaps pop a couple of bamboo mats over the top to provide filtered shade (like Lana did in her pool area on page 90).

Pre-pergola planning

Contrary to what some people think, pergolas may need council approval depending on their size, depth of footings, connection to the house, roof type, etc. Make sure you include a pergola in your original house plans.

THERE'S SO MUCH TO LOVE
ABOUT PERGOLAS ...

♥ They add dimension and depth to your home, particularly if the rear of your house has quite a flat vertical plane.

♥ They're pretty.

♥ They are quick and easy to build (and paint). A builder, landscaper or carpenter can do this for you.

♥ They're affordable.

♥ They suit many styles of home as pergolas can be made from different materials and designed with modern or traditional rafter shapes.

♥ They are also perfect for training plants. #starjasmine #ivy #bougainvillea

The beach shack

Polishing a *pearl* by the sea

Bon's family beach shack is hidden away in the heart of Pearl Beach on the Central Coast of New South Wales. It's a beautiful slice of the world, surrounded by tall trees and birds, that Bon and her family adore because of that mixture of beach vibe and rainforest. And although the shack is only small, it can comfortably accommodate three families with its open-plan living, high ceilings and outdoor spaces designed for entertaining kids and adults alike.

In its original '70s condition, this beach getaway was just a box with a tad too much brown and beige. It definitely needed a little TLC. Most of the year, the house is a rental, so we renovated it over a few different stages so that it wasn't off the market for too long. One of the first things we did was rip up the old carpet. We got lucky and discovered some beautiful pine floorboards underneath, which Bon's dad helped her to whitewash. #bonus! We then painted EVERYTHING white (no surprise there). Walls, ceilings and all of the original built-in cabinetry, you name it … no surface was spared.

Renovating the kitchen made a huge difference to the home's appeal, as did the new deck we built, with stadium-style stairs so all the guests could sit and watch the kids going crazy in the front yard. The Beach Shack is not delicate or too precious. It's fun, light-hearted, can get messy and is really easy to maintain. Everything in it is there to be used, sat on or drunk out of – there's even a bar cart for that much-needed wine time after a day at the beach.

BEFORE

Hello, Sunshine!
#BEACHLIFE

AFTER

PLEASE DON'T BUY TINY RUGS!

If you're buying a rug for a lounge room, it should be large enough to sit under the legs of your couch, with enough on either side to feel generous. You can also layer two different sized rugs on top of each other for a more textured finish, or overlap them to cover a large area if you need a cheaper option than one huge rug.

White paint
for days ♡

Bonnie

"Cypress pine floorboards can be found in many older homes and wannabe beach shacks. Often, they're hiding under some not-so-crash-hot carpet. Our advice? Rip up the carpet and whitewash those planks for an authentic coastal look which will stand the test of time. It's not hard to DIY; my dad and I did the floors at this house and they came up a treat."

IT'S 5 O'CLOCK SOMEWHERE!

A bar trolley is a movable party. It's a practical and pretty storage solution that can be positioned in the house like a piece of furniture … but it's ready to be wheeled out at a moment's notice to get the good times rolling. A bar cart or drinks trolley near your kitchen not only gives you extra storage, but it can also look divine and bring a relaxed holiday vibe to any home. Stock it with some good-looking glassware, a few bottles of your best and some fresh lemons and limes. It goes without saying that a roaming bar cart is NOT the best idea if you also have roaming toddlers! (Just imagine a little one testing out their new 'walker' while Mum and Dad aren't looking. #omg!)

Go a la carte

Bar carts aren't just for booze. Style them up with lush green plants, stacks of books, tea sets … if it's pretty, it's cart-worthy!

NEXT-GEN KITCHEN BENCH

The standard bench height in a kitchen is 900 mm but as generations get taller, so do benches. It's now quite common to find heights of 910–920 mm. It really comes down to personal preference.

IT'S ALL ABOUT A FLUSH FRIDGE

To avoid the dreaded 'fridge sticking out' problem (hey, it happens to the best of us), make sure you build your cabinetry deep enough. Fridges come in all different sizes, so you'll need to know which fridge you're buying before finalising your kitchen design. Your cabinetry will need to be between 700–850 mm deep to ensure a flush finish.

WE LOVE OPEN SHELVES BUT THEY CAN CRUCIFY A KITCHEN

If your open shelves become a home for dusty books, chipped, mismatched crockery and (dare we say it) colourful plastic bowls it's a #nooooo from us! Seriously guys, nothing ugly should ever be put on open shelves – that's what cupboards and drawers are for. Open shelves are for pretty things – they can be practical too – let's call them 'pretty practical'. We style our shelves with a combo of greenery, candles, books, canisters, stacked plates and bowls, and even artwork. Cluster items together in groups and make sure there are gaps between the groups. Don't overdo it – less is more. If you have multiple shelves, avoid putting crockery or glassware on the top shelf as it's likely to get dusty.

Retro cool

If you're not going to integrate your fridge, why not make a statement with it? There are several colourful and old-school cool designs to choose from. For this kitchen, we chose a mint-green fridge for a laid-back holiday vibe.

Good grout!

If you're using light-coloured grout on your splashback, make sure you seal it well to avoid it staining.

SPACE OUT YOUR SEATING

Squeezing too many stools under a bench is a no-no. Assume each stool needs to be around 50–60 cm wide to be comfortable and work back from there. A 2.4 metre-long island can handle four stools, an island 1.8 metres long can have three. Avoid stools that are more than 70 cm in height, as this can make for a tight squeeze between the thighs and the benchtop! Around 65 cm in height is ideal for a stool. And the benchtop overhang required for comfy seating is between 300 and 450 mm.

TAKE THE INSIDE OUTSIDE

The best outside spaces are seamless extensions of the interior. So, when styling your outside space(s), it's a good idea to borrow many of the same principles you used inside your house and execute them using outdoor-worthy products. Take inspiration from the colour schemes you've used indoors, particularly in any rooms adjacent to the alfresco space, and carry those through to the outside. Here, the rope chairs we used in the dining space are picked up again outside on the deck, and the blues and greens in the outdoor cushions complement the colours used in the lounge room on the other side of those French doors.

DON'T RELY ON MOONLIGHT

Lighting is frequently forgotten when designing outdoor spaces, but if you get it right, it adds atmosphere and can extend your entertaining hours well into the night (sorry, neighbours!) to really maximise your alfresco space. #hellowinetime! You should plan your exterior lighting at the same time you develop your landscaping and alfresco plans. Your electrician will need to know exactly where you want lights to go so they can 'rough in' the electricals while your home is under construction. And either you or your electrician will also need to source lights that are suitable and safe for the type of outdoor use you're after.

TRY THIS AT HOME

Once the sun goes down, grab a torch and stand outside in the space that you're turning into your dream alfresco area. If you currently have outside lights in that space, turn them on. If not, just stand there in the dark. Try to visualise what lighting you would like to have to make this your dream outdoor space. What do you want to see? For example:

♥ Do you have some grass that you'd like the kids to be able to play on, even after dark? If so, a few well-directed spotlights mounted on the eaves at the back of your house could be just what you need.

♥ Is there a feature in your yard you'd like to draw attention to; a beautiful tree, perhaps, or an architectural wall? In that case, some accent lighting (think uplights) that draws attention to those features might be a good idea.

♥ Can you see all the way to your back fence? Would you like to? Lighting to the back boundary can make a yard look and feel bigger at night.

♥ If you (and your guests) use the side access of your house, is there adequate lighting along the paths so you aren't stumbling through the dark?

Once you've considered all of these things, walk around the outdoor area, using your torch if necessary, to nut out exactly what lighting you think you need.

FLIP TIP

Don't throw too much money at outdoor lighting as most buyers will view your house during the day and struggle to adequately value the investment you've made on outdoor lights.

USING ART FOR IMPACT

- Because this house is by the beach, we wanted to use some stunning underwater artwork in the bedrooms to bring the coastal theme to life.
- When choosing artwork, you need to ask yourself this basic question: Do I want the colours in the piece of art to 'complement' or 'contrast' the rest of the room? The two underwater pieces contrast the whites of the rooms, while the large piece we went for in the guest cottage complements the blush tones of the linens and the rose gold vase.
- Don't forget to consider the frame. This important detail needs to work with both the art AND the surrounding colours used in the room. Black or white frames are safe options that look good anywhere, plus they won't go out of fashion like metallic frames might. We love pale oak timber frames but you do need to ensure the timber works with any other timber elements in the room (especially if you have timber floors).
- There are some really affordable artwork options out there, which look stunning. Lots of mainstream furniture stores now have a great range and you can even search by price point. Or, if you're keen on an artist, buying a digital print of theirs instead of an original will also help your budget.
- How big should the artwork be? There's nothing worse than a piece of art too small for the space it's in. If you're unsure about size, tape some joined pieces of paper up on the wall to help you get a sense of scale and determine what size you need. If in doubt, go a bit bigger.

DECIDE ON THE FOCAL POINT

Knowing what the focal point of a room is going to be before you style it is really important. The focal point can be a structural element, like a picture window, or it can be a piece of statement furniture or something else, like the artwork we used in the master suite (right) and the guest bedroom (above). A focal point typically sets itself apart from the rest of the room because of its scale, colour or texture. We like to think about the focal point of each room very early on in a reno because it helps us work out where we're going to build a structural focal point, or where we need to put a statement piece of furniture to create a focal point.

Guest cottage ♡

THE MORE, THE MERRIER

Holiday homes come to life with family and friends, so being able to accommodate lots of little people is key. Despite being a small room, the central window here allows space for a set of bunk beds on either side.

Our rookie reno

Learning curves *ahead!*

Talk about a baptism by fire! Our first renovation was as challenging as it gets. We planned to buy the worst house in the suburb and flip it for a pretty profit in just six weeks. As soon as we set foot on this property for our first viewing, the stench hit our nostrils and we thought, 'This house stinks – it's perfect!' We knew that most people would be scared off by its poor condition, so we were in with a real chance of buying it at a good price. And we did.

Because it was filled to the brim with rubbish, accomplishing even the most basic of tasks was tough. We had to guess some of the sizes of the rooms because we couldn't get the tape measure from wall to wall. It was very dark inside and the front yard was so overgrown that you couldn't see the house from the street. One neighbour told us she'd been looking at the same bed sheet hanging on the Hills Hoist for a decade. Talk about a bad view!

But it was the run-down condition of the house that made it so rewarding to renovate. The changes were rapid as we knocked out walls to create an open-plan design that was light, breezy and modern. We were even able to save the original floorboards.

The neighbours loved us. They told us that in just six weeks the house had gone from an eyesore to the best house in the street. Locals were honking their horns and stopping their cars to tell us how much they loved and appreciated what we were doing. It was an unexpected perk of this particular reno.

BEFORE

AFTER

BEFORE

Keep that green pristine!

Always lay your turf last to protect it.

AFTER

BEFORE

AFTER

Erin

"There's no denying it ... rendering over bricks delivers the greatest exterior transformation – but rendering a whole home can cost a packet. We've found one of the best ways to update an ugly brick exterior is by spraying the bricks using a premium exterior paint. It's much cheaper and can be done in 1–2 days by a professional, or you can tackle it yourself. If you've got your heart set on that rendered look, you can render just the front façade and spray the sides and back to match, like we did here."

LET'S TALK TURF

If you can increase the amount of green grass out the front or back of your house, DO IT! It will make your home look more appealing. #moneybackguarantee You may need to clear away a few dead or dying bushes, but the end result will be so much stronger with a neat patch of turf out front. Our landscapers built a white picket fence, then we laid the new turf ourselves over a weekend and voila! The old barren front garden was transformed into a beautiful new yard, perfect for a family.

A CLEVER FLOORPLAN HAS THE ABILITY TO CHANGE YOUR LIFE

Improving the floorplan of a house is the FIRST thing we look at when we're renovating. Reimagining a floorplan can make the biggest difference to the way a house looks and feels, and it can also be an expensive thing to fix if you don't get it right the first time.

REMOVING WALLS ISN'T SCARY

Most older houses were built with lots of separate rooms. It's just the way things were done back then. Open-plan living wasn't even a concept and many thought 'alfresco' was a pizza topping. When planning your reno, remember that some of the walls will be load-bearing (holding up your house). If removing those walls is the key to your plan, you'll likely have to factor in extra time (and money) to put structural beams in the ceiling to replace them.

TO KEEP, OR NOT TO KEEP?

Original flooring can present a real dilemma. If you're renovating adjoining rooms and plan to remove walls, it might be difficult to keep the original timber flooring — you'll need to patch the floor where the walls used to be. This can be costly and challenging if you're after a seamless look for your floors. You may also be forced to lay a plank running in the opposite direction of the existing floors to fill the gap left by the wall.

The river shack

Our *tiniest* reno ever!

This River Shack reno was a totally unique challenge for us and, quite literally, it is our tiniest reno to date! A dilapidated little caravan set on the bank of a river formed the backbone of this build. Over the years, a shack had been hammered up out the front of the caravan, and we wanted to combine these two elements into one ultimate weekender – a place where you could retreat from the stresses of grown-up life and really let your hair down. And we knew from the get-go that we were going to experiment with colour. #yeswayrosé

Up until this reno, we'd painted most of our walls white. In fact, we still tend to paint our ceilings, walls and trims the same colour. #whiteonwhiteonwhite (Did we happen to mention we love white?) But we put our love affair with white on hold because we knew this shack was the perfect opportunity to branch out of our comfort zone. Why? Because it's a weekender!

Thankfully, the design rules of everyday life don't apply to a weekender. It should feel like an escape and what better way to create that feeling than to be adventurous with colour? We went bold, got creative (#cabinfever) and couldn't be happier with how it turned out.

Because this tiny house sees a lot of action, we focused on budget buys, super-durable materials and multi-function furnishings. Now it has heaps of personality and cool space-saving and storage solutions. Every single nook and cranny is living its best life. It's bold, it's black … and we absolutely love it!

BEFORE

AFTER

HAVE FUN WITH MATERIALS

If you're building from scratch or adding an extension to your home, lucky you! You have the option to use new materials and aren't locked into transforming the existing ones. This reno is a great example of having some fun with new materials. We built the framework extension to accommodate the vertically grooved fibre-cement sheeting. This Scyon Axon cladding creates a strong visual impact with its modern clean lines, and once we painted it black (literally, the paint colour is Black by Dulux), our modern bush cabin was complete. One of the huge benefits of using fibre-cement cladding instead of timber is how resistant it is to rot, fire and termites – basically everything a house is vulnerable to in the bush by the river.

UPCYLE OLD WINDOWS!

Try to re-use windows and doors wherever possible. We upcycled these old windows from Lana's Forever Home renovation, painted them black and gave them a second lease of life here.

COLOURS FOR A WEEKENDER

The colour scheme that's suitable for a holiday home you only visit now and then can be quite different from the one you might choose for your Forever Home. The stakes are much lower, so you have a real opportunity to play and experiment with something that makes you happy. We had heaps of fun with our colour choices on this reno, both inside and out, as you can probably tell from the blush pink and black caravan with lightning bolt, and the strelitzia wallpaper.

Caravan dreams

What do you do with an old caravan you aren't ready to part with? Build a modern shack around it, obviously! We clad the inside of this old girl in Axon, wrapped wallpaper to die for onto the ceiling and turned her into a luxe little lady.

HOLIDAY SAVER

When decking out a caravan, it's hard to find bunk beds that will fit the space. These needed to be custom-made by our builder. Sounds expensive, you're thinking? But it was the opposite. Our guy knocked these cuties up using plywood before we could say 'kids into bed'. And the best bit? We included some sneaky storage under the bottom mattress to store extra bed linen.

Bonnie

"I love the Axon cladding we used for the outside of the shack so much, I had to use it inside as well. I put it in every room except the bathroom, and I love how it turned out. It adds texture and interest and gives this house that holiday cabin feeling – way more fun than generic plasterboard."

Black bombshell

This is the smallest kitchen we've created, and it's one of our favourites. It's little, with a BIG personality. We stained the timber veneer cabinets black, to give it a sleek, modern look and match the exterior of the shack.

Whenever we place a **timber table on timber-look flooring**, we like to break up the visual with a rug, to avoid timber on timber and to add another layer of texture to the room.

IS BLACK THE NEW WHITE?

No. White will always reign supreme in kitchens, however black is still a popular choice among designers and DIYers alike. It sounds counterintuitive, but black is actually an obvious alternative to white. White is beautiful largely because of its simplicity and neutrality. The same can be said of black, it's just at the opposite end of the spectrum, though black is better when it comes to adding richness and depth. Done right, it oozes style, sophistication and drama. A decision to be made in parallel with this one is whether to go black-on-black – with black cabinetry and black benchtops, like we did here – or to go for contrast in the form of a white or timber benchtop.

DARK CAN BE DELICATE

Dark cabinets need a bit more TLC than light ones because scratches, dings, dust and fingerprints tend to show more easily. Consider a textured finish (like a wood grain) to help counteract this.

MATT BLACK GOES MAINSTREAM

A matt black finish on tapware has made its way into the mainstream and offers a gorgeous and relatively conservative alternative to chrome. It's affordable and doesn't have the long lead times some of the other coloured finishes have. The best bit is that black looks great with almost any kitchen colour scheme and style but just be aware that it can fade and it shouldn't be cleaned with any chemicals (just soapy water).

WHY CHOOSE A SINGLE SINK?

For those of us with limited space or another sink in a butler's pantry, a single sink can be a winner. Interestingly, you'll often find a single sink can fit large pots and pans better than a double sink can. Even though a double is wider overall, the two bowls are usually smaller individually.

ART IN A KITCHEN WORKS!

Cooking can be quite the creative process, so it makes sense to have an inspiring piece of art hanging nearby. The obvious constraint is where to find the space to hang art in a kitchen amid all the cabinetry. We'll admit hanging art won't work for everyone, but if there is a side wall or an open shelf you can lean a print on, it's worth considering. We intentionally designed this kitchen with no overhead cupboards in order to make the small kitchen feel as open as possible. This allowed us to hang a statement piece of art above the bench. This print ties in with the overall theme of the shack — an eclectic combo of masculine and feminine energy. A car burnout never looked so pretty. #grittypretty

IF YOU HAVE A SMALL KITCHEN …

- Opt for the smallest appliances available, like a skinny 30 cm cooktop or single DishDrawer (we love these) instead of a full dishwasher.
- Integrate appliances if your budget allows – doing this will make the kitchen feel larger and look less disjointed (see pages 27 and 200 for more).
- Steer clear of any overhead cabinets; they can close the space in.
- Go for a dining table in place of an island bench. You can still prep food there if you need to.
- Consider an indoor/outdoor servery – it definitely makes this kitchen feel bigger than it actually is.

Storage-friendly sinks

If space is at a premium in your kitchen, look for a sink with the drain at the back (rather than in the centre of the bowl). The plumbing will take up less space in the cupboard underneath, giving you more space for storage.

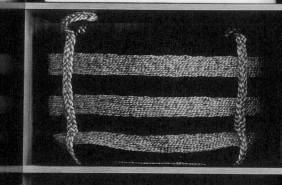

Euro laundry and an integrated fridge

TIGHT ON SPACE? SAY BONJOUR TO THE EURO LAUNDRY

The Europeans created this 'laundry in a cupboard' idea in response to their slightly tighter living quarters, but now we Aussies are stealing it with pride whenever we find ourselves in a spatial jam. At Three Birds, we're big fans of the compact nature of this arrangement, and we also love the convenience it provides when located in the right spot. Being connected to a kitchen or bathroom makes it super easy to access while doing other things. This one is so close to the kitchen you can literally put on a load of washing while making some toast. It's also one of the smallest laundries we've ever built at only 700 mm wide x 650 mm deep x 2200 mm tall!

If you love top-loader washing machines, this might not be the best solution for you. Most space-efficient Euro laundries have a front-loader washing machine under the bench. You can then either stack a dryer on top for a tall, skinny laundry, or, if you have the width, put the dryer and washer side-by-side under the counter for maximum bench space. If you can fit in a sink, that's ideal but it's not essential. You'll also need some storage space for your laundry detergent, perhaps an ironing board too, if you can fit it in. Most importantly, don't forget to put an exhaust fan and light in the cupboard to keep it cool and dry – a condensing dryer will help reduce the vented moisture when drying clothes. (Full disclaimer: We didn't end up putting a fan or a light in this laundry – the cost involved was a bit steep for this weekender. On the rare occasions the dryer gets used, Bon simply leaves the cupboard door open.)

WASHING WEEKEND BODIES

Of course, outdoor showers are pretty practical for washing off sand and salt, but they're also unbeatable for creating a coastal vibe. And if you can hook it up to hot water, that's a bonus everyone will appreciate!

Erin

"It's crucial to consider how your fixtures and fittings will work together in a bathroom. In this reno, we had already roughed in a rail shower before Bon realised the long vertical rail would prevent her from putting the wall mixer where she wanted it – centred and aligned with the basin mixer. The only solution? Change to an overhead rain shower, which meant re-doing the rough in. This cost us time and money. As the saying goes, the devil's in the detail."

TINY BATHROOMS CAN STILL BRING THE WOW!

Start by getting a handle on the overall size of the box (or matchbox) you've got to work with. Some lucky ducks might have a generous size of 8 square metres or larger to work with for their bathroom, but most will be working in a tighter space. Looking back at the bathrooms we've renovated, the average size for a main bathroom has been under 8 square metres, and about half that for an ensuite. There are pros and cons to both. Of course, having a large bathroom is nice, but costs increase accordingly once all the pretty tiling goes in to that big space. The good news is that a well-designed bathroom can be a total stunner, large or small.

DARK OR LIGHT?

If you're unsure about whether or not to go with light or dark tiles in your bathroom, remember that light coloured or neutral tiles will always make a space look larger and they will also make your bathroom feel more open, spacious and bright. Dark tiles can introduce a sophisticated mood as well as drama – and while a darker tile can make your bathroom appear smaller, you can break the rules like we did here. It wasn't a big space but we decided to prioritise creating the right retro vibe by using the pink and black tiles ahead of making it look larger. No regrets!

SQUARE TILES AIN'T FOR SQUARES

In fact, square tiles come in so many cool colours and finishes these days they can be a game changer in a bathroom – like these pink tiles (which we mixed up in a matt and a gloss finish). At the other end of the colour spectrum, we also love basic white 100 mm square tiles laid in a brick pattern. They're perfect when you need a budget option that won't distract from the feature tile. The same goes for large, simple 600 mm square floor tiles in a matt finish. Still not convinced about the squares? Head to page 206 for more square flair.

Nude grout!

LOUNGE ROOM STYLING: A FEW KEY POINTERS

- **Create balance:** Be sure to balance high and low pieces as well as heavy and light ones around the room.

- **Bigger couches aren't always better:** Many people fall into the trap of taking measurements of their room, then buying the biggest possible couch to fit it. Not only will that make it hard to move around the space, it will also make the room look smaller, not bigger. Don't do this, we beg you! If in doubt, go smaller rather than too big; you can always add a side table or pouf to pad it out but you can't shrink a couch (not yet, anyway!).

- **Fabric choice is very important:** Especially in a weekend getaway like this one, where relaxing and spending time as a family is so important. Consider who will be using the room – toddlers with sticky hands or just you and your hubbie? Choose a fabric that will last longer than a weekend.

- **Splurge vs. save:** Decide on the big-ticket items you will spend on – these will be your investment pieces – versus others you plan to refresh much sooner.

- **Finishes:** Many furniture items include accents of timber or metallics. These could be the legs of a sofa or frame of a glass coffee table. The colour of these accents needs to be in keeping with the rest of the choices in the room. But that doesn't mean you can't mix metallics, like we did. If you go for timber legs, make sure they'll work with any timber floors in the space.

- **Flexibility:** The best designed rooms are ones that can be manipulated to accommodate a few different scenarios, so keep this in mind when picking furniture. Perhaps a crowd of people have stopped by or you want to be able to relax looking out a certain window. In this house, a swivel chair is the perfect choice as it allows for facing towards the couch, the kitchen or even the river.

Be a rebel!

USE AN OUTDOOR LIGHT INSIDE

Gotta love a floor lamp! Sure, they give a nice glowing ambient light, but they also look really good and bring height to a room. Choose a lamp made of materials that suit the other elements around it, like this metallic beauty. And don't forget to install dimmers in the rest of the room for a gentle ambient glow. You'll thank us later!

Fold-out bed!

THINK MULTIPURPOSE

If you're tight on space (or even if you're not), go for built-ins and pieces of furniture that are multifunctional. Not only does the built-in daybed double as a bed (Bon created storage for bedding and linen underneath, of course!), but the unassuming grey ottoman next to it also folds out into yet another bed.

MAKE THE MOST OF EVERY NOOK

The multifunction philosophy continues in this dining nook, where we added built-in bench seating that doubles as storage. It's not big, but we can squeeze a surprising amount of hungry kids around this table. And when everyone's finished, the table can be pushed in and the stools tucked under to free up more floor space.

Surprise! Vinyl's back!

Vinyl ain't what it used to be. Today's vinyl planks look like timber and are the ideal choice for a weekender. They're water-resistant and able to withstand all of that holiday action.

If you've been keeping track, you know that we've built HardieDecks at most of our renovations. They're so damn durable, and they can be painted any colour under the sun. **We usually choose white or light grey, but we stained this deck to look like timber** – it suits the bush surrounds and camouflages any little muddy footprints.

PRETTY AND PRACTICAL

In the renovating world, there are few things 'as pretty as a picture' window, or as practical. Add a bench seat to a glass pane and you not only create an aesthetically pleasing box around the window, you also create a great spot to sit and enjoy the view.

ALFRESCO ENVY

If your home doesn't have an alfresco area, we bet there's an opportunity to create one somewhere – even if it's small. The best alfresco areas are built directly off an open-plan living space and kitchen. Please don't consider a patch of grass around the side of the house your alfresco solution! It needs to be connected to inside and easily accessible. As you know by now, an indoor/outdoor servery with large windows that allows people to sit outside while still socialising with those inside is one of our favourite solutions.

YEARNING FOR BI-FOLDS?

If you are seriously hamstrung by your budget, traditional bi-fold doors might be out of reach, but don't worry! You can hinge together some regular doors, like we did here. These don't run on a track, so they won't last forever, but they're so cheap you will probably be able to afford to replace them every few years.

WE LOVE A GOOD BANANA PALM

They add just the right touch of tropical calm to pretty much any space. Remember that the pot or vessel you choose for your plant can make just as much of an impact as the plant itself. Indoors, we like to use simple pots in whites and metallics, and rattan-coloured baskets, whereas outside we find it hard to go past bold patterns. And always upsize your pot – bigger is usually better.

177

Modern coastal barn

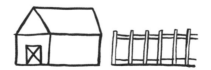

Bonnie's *dream* home

Welcome to the home that Bonnie's been dreaming about for over a decade, and planning for the last five years. Growing up with parents who lived a 'buy, renovate and sell' lifestyle meant Bon moved houses more than most. As inconvenient as that sounds, she absorbed so much invaluable knowledge along the way. You could say she's been surrounded by reno inspo her whole life (well before Pinterest was invented), and she's been cataloguing ideas in her mind of what SHE would do one day, if it were her home! Well, that day eventually came ...

Bonnie's vision was clear – she wanted a modern coastal barn. This style combines her long love affair with the coastal look, with her connection to the great outdoors and the farming lifestyle. Bon's husband, Nathan, grew up in the Southern Highlands, so having land and lots of space has always been important to him. All she had to do was work her reno magic to bring those coastal vibes inland by about 25 kilometres.

Choosing the look for the exterior of any home is a massive decision as it sets the tone for the entire house. For Bon, this decision was made many moons ago – it had to be white weatherboard. But the ultimate motivation behind the design and style of Bonnie's Dream Home was creating a haven for her and Nathan, their four boys, the dogs, cows, and as many friends and family as their hearts desire. The plan was to renovate and extend the existing brick house, but major structural problems forced a knock-down-rebuild. #holyplanB!

BEFORE

AFTER

LIGHT-LOVER'S PARADISE

Glass windows and doors were always going to be a major feature of Bonnie's Dream Home. She's a light-lover and that's exactly what your windows and doors are there for – to let in light. Windows and doors form the foundation of how a space feels, and if you miss the mark here, no amount of rugs and karate-chopped cushions can right that wrong.

THINK ABOUT THE EXTERIOR

Of course, you see windows from inside your home, but their position also affects the look of the exterior. We usually plan where we want them from an internal perspective first (for that all-important natural light), then consider what they will look like from the outside to make sure that's the look we want.

GLASS IS NOT JUST GLASS

This is where we get really excited because hopefully we're about to teach you something you didn't know about glass. Not that long ago, we thought glass was glass. It's see-through, you clean it with Windex. No big deal, right? How wrong we were! Turns out there are different types of glass you can put in your windows and doors to make your home more comfortable. There's glass to reduce heat loss in winter, reduce UV glare in summer and minimise noise all year round. We like to use glass everywhere! We're slightly obsessed with natural light, so to ensure we build comfortable homes, we go through the process of choosing and specifying the glass we want with our window company to ensure the right glass gets included in the quotes.

ALUMINIUM OR TIMBER FRAMES?

This is an important decision you'll have to make for your windows and doors. Bonnie loves the look of timber and also how it makes her feel (ah, the romance!), but you might not have a choice. In Australia and other parts of the world, the threat of bushfire is very real, and homes need to be built accordingly. Depending on the BAL (Bushfire Attack Level) rating of your house, you might not be allowed to have timber frames. This was the case on this build. Bonnie had to use aluminium frames along the back of her house, which is BAL 40 rated. At the front of her house, she was able to use timber. Despite having both types of frame in her house they look absolutely fine together. Aluminium windows are cheaper to buy, install and maintain than timber, and they now come in loads of sleek designs with great powder-coated finishes, so are definitely worth considering.

SPACE-AGE ROOFING?

It's no longer just about terracotta or slate, there's a new kid on the block – a composite roof material called Elemental. It can be used on a lower pitch roof than normal tiles, and is made from an advanced material originally developed for aerospace (oh hi, NASA!). It's not metal, so it can withstand Australia's harshest weather conditions without rusting, denting or blowing away. As if that weren't enough, it can be ordered in all different colours and sizes.

Erin

"Ordering windows should be at the top of your to-do list, purely because they have long lead times and can delay your whole reno if you don't order them early enough. Without your windows, your home won't be watertight, meaning you can't insulate or sheet the interior walls or do anything else, as things may get wet. This means you're pretty much STUCK and unable to progress any further until windows can be installed – and this can blow your timeline and your budget."

Bonnie created a decorative chevron pattern in the front entry

FLOORING FIRST

Even though new flooring is one of the last items to go down in a new house or major renovation, it's one of the earliest decisions you need to make because you need to know the exact thickness of your floorboards, tiles or carpet in order to ensure you construct the house with these finished floor heights in mind. Being out on that measurement by even a few millimetres can mean having unsightly gaps under doors or, at the other end of the spectrum, doors that drag on the carpet. Don't rush your choice of flooring. It helps set the mood and vibe of your home, you'll walk on it every day AND it usually absorbs a big chunk of your reno budget, so you want to get it right.

OUR ENGINEERED TIMBER CRUSH

Bonnie chose engineered timber flooring from Woodcut. We absolutely love engineered timber floorboards – they're the best option for anyone wanting real timber, but a more stable and durable version of it. Engineered timber is real timber, just made up of layers. Think of it like a sandwich: the top piece of bread is what you see. It's about 6 mm of real hardwood timber, like a European or American oak. The middle and bottom slices of the sandwich are packed with goodness – either a softwood like poplar or a man-made core. This makes the whole sandwich super strong and stable. This type of timber can be sanded and refinished for a refresh of colour or an entirely new stain.

ALL HAIL THE HIGH CEILING!

Ceilings may not have a reputation for being the most exciting element of a room, but they should get more attention. Geez, they can make a big difference. Here are a few structural things to consider when evaluating the ceiling styles in your house:

❤ **Height** Apparently, high ceilings are one of the most coveted features by people looking to buy a house. The higher, the better we say. What's not to love about high ceilings? They immediately make a room feel more spacious and airy. And did you know that some research shows that high ceilings promote clearer thinking, higher energy levels and overall happiness. (Say whaaat? No wonder we love them!) The only downside to high ceilings is that noise can bounce around a bit more and it does take longer to heat the space, but these things can be managed by adding some soft surfaces in the room to help absorb sound and by ensuring the ceiling, and the rest of the walls are well insulated.

❤ **Vaulted** Most ceilings are flat, but they don't need to be. You may be able to create a vaulted or pitched ceiling, which follows the angles of your roof to create a 'loft-style' feel. Don't think every room needs the same treatment – we often vault ceilings in one or two rooms to make a feature out of them.

❤ **Rafters** Exposing the roof rafters adds an authentic touch, especially when combined with a vaulted ceiling. If you can't expose your rafters for whatever reason, ask your builder to create cosmetic ones, like Bonnie did here. They're just pieces of timber stuck onto the ceiling but they make a big impact.

Matchy matchy!

We always tint our ceiling paint to match the colour of the walls.

#KEEPITSIMPLE

Styling a space isn't a green light to clutter up a gorgeous room with loads of stuff. Trust us, clutter will accumulate over time so the less you start with, the better. A few well-chosen items is plenty. Don't overdo it.

WHAT'S YOUR STYLING PLAN?

Don't wait until your reno has finished to think about how you're going to style the new space. We know it can be almost impossible to imagine what your finished house will look like when it resembles a bombsite, but it's great to get a head start on what will go where once your renovation is finally complete. And you may find your favourite furniture choices have three-month lead times, so place your orders as soon as you can and you will be ready to turn that bombsite into a home as soon as you see the back of the construction cleaners.

COUCH SURFING

Before buying a couch, we immerse ourselves in our inspo pics and browse online to see what suits the style of home we're trying to create. We look at the colours in our inspo pics as well as any defining features on the 'body' of the sofa. Does it have a high or low back? Wide or skinny arms? How much leg is showing? Will it work as an L-shape?

FUTURE-PROOF YOUR FABRICS

Spills and stains are bound to happen to any sofa. In our experience, adults are just as deadly with a glass of vin rouge in their hand as a toddler with an uncapped red marker. If you can choose a washable fabric without compromising on style and colour, that's a real win.

FOAM OR FEATHERS?

High-quality foam is a great choice for a sofa as it's less expensive and more durable than feathers, so your sofa will always look 'fluffed'. Feather-filled cushions on the other hand give that luxurious, 'sink into' feeling, but be prepared to fluff, puff and pouf those cushions daily! We think the ideal solution is a combo deal of foam and feathers.

CREATE ESCAPES

The proliferation of open-plan living can create the need for secondary spaces where family members can retreat from the main hustle and bustle of the home. Keep in mind who is most likely to use these rooms – kids or adults –and then furnish them to suit.

REMEMBER, FAMILIES GROW UP

If you're undertaking a significant reno on the home you plan to live in for a long time, creating a floorplan that will also work in 10 to 15 years is a must. You might have toddlers now, but how will the house function when they're teenagers? In their early years, you'll probably want the playroom under your nose – near the kitchen, perhaps. But once they become teenagers, you (and your kids) will prefer they have somewhere else to escape to in the house. Perhaps you don't have kids yet, but are planning a family? Consider those future needs today and you'll avoid major headaches down the track.

WELCOME TO BONNIE'S GUEST COTTAGE

Granny flats are starting to pop up in loads of Aussie backyards to accommodate elderly parents, older children reluctant to leave the nest, or to provide a source of rental income. Bonnie's guest cottage is connected to the main house but still has its own front door and distinctive style.

HOW TO HANDLE A TALL AND SKINNY BATHROOM

♥ **Go built-in (inset) for the bath:** You'll find this style of bath in most homes that need renovating, but that doesn't mean it's not worthy of modern-day renovations – it can be. Bonnie put a built-in bath in this bathroom. They are great for tight, squeezy spaces and designed to be wedged into a room, making them perfect for narrow bathrooms that might only be 1500 mm wide.

♥ **Add a skylight:** Allowing natural light into a long, skinny room that might otherwise be dark is a great way of creating the feeling of more space.

♥ **Create a 'wet zone':** 'What's a wet zone?' you ask. The beauty of a wet zone is that it allows you to squeeze a shower and a bath into a smaller space. A standard shower size is 900 x 900 mm, which is ample space, until you put a door on and then you feel like you're showering in a phone booth (no thanks!). Walk-in showers are growing in popularity, but they often take up more space because they have no door. If you're going for a walk-in, your shower screen really needs to be a minimum of 1000 mm long (ideally 1200 mm) to keep water spray under control. We haven't had the space for a full-size walk-in shower in a couple of our renos, and this was one of them. Our solution in those instances is to create a wet zone instead, and pop the shower and the bath behind a shower screen.

DON'T BE AFRAID OF COLOUR

By now, you've noticed that we really love white, but we also love using colour when it's right for a room. Colour is one of the key elements of design to consider when renovating. It doesn't matter how much time and money you spend on finishes, materials, flooring, tiles and the like – if you don't get the colour right, you won't be happy with the result. To give the cottage its own identity, Bon chose this deep emerald green, called Frontier by Dulux, for a feature wall. Not only did it draw attention to the stunning cladding, it also made the peak of the raked ceiling more noticeable than if it were white on white. It makes the room.

Beaten brass beauty. We love the tap in this wet bar. Did you know that most taps in the world are brass? They are just coated in chrome plating and other finishes to hide the brass. This is why brass taps are sometimes called uncoated.

YOU CAN HAVE YOUR OWN BAR!

If you like the idea of having a bar in your home but you aren't sure you've got the space, it might be easier than you think to fit one in. Gone are the days where you need a 'walk around bar' to stand behind, like in a pub. In our experience, that type of set-up requires too much space. All you really need is an indent in a wall to put a benchtop, and maybe some cabinets if the budget can stretch to that. A working sink is a definite plus, but you don't even need that to kick off happy hour (check out the bar we built in The New Classic on page 116).

Take in the view

Positioning a desk so it faces a windowless wall might seem like a sensible plan, but it's not a very inspiring outlook. Much better to arrange the furniture so your back is against the wall and you are facing the room.

#SITLIKEABOSS

Formal dining

Family dining

DINING DONE TWO WAYS

Dining tables bring family and friends together, and when you've got a big family, like Bonnie, don't hold back on creating not one, but two dining spaces. There's the formal dining room, which can be closed off with glass doors, and then there's the family dining table, which has a more relaxed communal feel to it. Both Bon and Lana chose round dining tables for their homes – they're practical, space-efficient and easy to style.

199

BONNIE ♥S THIS KITCHEN!

This kitchen is truly the heart of Bonnie's Dream Home (it really is the holy grail of kitchens!). As Bruno Mars would say, Bonnie is 'hashtag blessed'. Even though she absolutely loved our mint green kitchen in the Cottage with a Modern Twist, the grey cabinetry in The New Classic and The River Shack's black-on-black kitchen, her Dream Home's kitchen was always going to be white – always. Why?

INTEGRATE WHERE YOU CAN

Can you spot the appliances? It's tough because they've all been integrated seamlessly behind the custom cabinetry. We are massive fans of integrated appliances, and it's always on our kitchen wish lists. No matter what style of kitchen you're after, concealing a fridge and dishwasher behind seamless cabinetry is usually going to look better than the alternative – except perhaps if you've bought a coloured fridge to make a statement, like we did for The Beach Shack (page 139). But integrated appliances will cost quite a bit more, so your budget might make the decision for you.

IF YOU WANT TO SAVE ON YOUR BENCHTOP…

We reckon 20 mm thickness is a good choice; it will keep costs down because it is a standard size, yet it's still thick enough to minimise chips and breaks. You'll have to make a decision about the thickness of your benchtop early in the kitchen design process, because it will affect how your cabinetry is built.

WHY BONNIE CHOSE WHITE

01

It's timeless – no matter what colour trends there are for kitchens, white will always be #1 on any popularity chart in the world.

02

White makes us feel wonderful – happy, relaxed, clean and fresh … like we're on holidays by the beach.

03

It suits the overall home. Bon's inspo pics for a 'modern coastal barn' are awash with white so she chose a colour that suited the style of her home. Remember, tying the kitchen's look and feel to the overall theme you are going for is so important when choosing colours for your kitchen.

04

White is a blank canvas – there are no limitations on Bonnie in terms of how she can style her kitchen in the future. When working with white, the world is your oyster.

So … which white?

If you're going for a custom kitchen you may want to match the cabinetry to the white on your walls. Bonnie opted for Dulux White on White for both her walls and her kitchen. It's a cool white that feels crisp and clean.

Now that's a chandelier you can swing from!

In Bon's kitchen, a row of multiple pendants was never going to cut it above that island bench. She'd had her eye on this 'Cloud' chandelier for a long time. At 1.4 metres wide, it's the perfect accent piece for her statement kitchen, hanging slightly off-centre over the island.

Holy mother of benchtops!

Forget what's in fashion, Bon knows what she likes, and she
wanted a big, fat, chunky apron of stone for her kitchen benchtop.
She went for a 300 mm thickness while the rest of the world was
moving in the other direction with ultra-thin 12 mm benchtops.
And guess what? She loves it and so do we!

You can use Axon cladding as a splashback. It's waterproof and heat resistant!

OUR FIRST BUTLER'S PANTRY

Most butler's pantries (BPs) aren't as big as Bon's, but they serve the same purpose: they're a second smaller space to store things you'd prefer not be seen in the main kitchen, and to perform certain tasks. Bonnie went for a full kit-out in her BP, including a large sink, an extra oven (perfect when catering for big family get-togethers or parties) and an integrated fridge. There's also open shelving to keep the room feeling nice and airy.

BPs ARE GREAT FOR HIDING...

- clunky benchtop appliances (think Thermomix, blender, soda stream, toaster or slow-cooker);
- microwaves;
- dirty dishes;
- food prep for parties;
- post-party mess you can't face tackling; and
- any paperwork that doesn't have a proper home yet.

AND IF YOU LOVE ENTERTAINING…

A butler's pantry can be a great spot to prepare and store extra food when you're having a party. If you're flash enough to have caterers handling the festivities it's a great area for them to set up and work out of. When choosing fixtures and finishes for your butler's pantry, you need to consider how much of it can be seen from the main kitchen. If it's quite visible, your choices should complement or match the space outside it. Our advice is don't make this room too visible or what's the point? It's supposed to hide stuff!

Including a butler's pantry in your kitchen design will cost you additional cashola, but you may be able to choose cheaper fixtures and fittings if they're not clearly visible from the main kitchen. Having said that, be careful not to go 'cheap and nasty' – you still want to enjoy the space and it needs to stand the torture test of all the mess. Not using cupboard fronts in this area will save you dollars.

SUPER-SIZED SERVERY

We've put indoor/outdoor serveries in all of our renos so of course it was on Bon's wish list too. She opted for bi-fold windows (a necessity for an opening this size) instead of a gas-strut, and also decided to pop a small second sink into the kitchen side of the servery so she could wash up and watch the kids in the pool at the same time.

IS TAPWARE FAST FASHION?

We think it could be! At least that's what some people believe, and it makes sense because, unlike many other fixtures and design decisions, tapware can be updated easily, much like a seasonal wardrobe. Personally, we think that's a bit OTT, but compared to benchtops and cabinetry, it is true that your kitchen sink mixer is the first place you should look if you're planning to do a quick refresh of your kitchen. And let's be real, now that there are so many more choices beyond classic chrome, we're all a little bit eager to try something new.

Lana

"Gone are the days when only tradies could access a huge range of tapware at great prices. With the expansion of online shopping, you can (and should) take on that responsibility yourself by finding the items you like and ordering them direct. This removes the mark-up your tradie would have passed on to you, not to mention their charge for the time spent sourcing and buying them."

YOU'RE EITHER A LAUNDRY PERSON OR YOU'RE NOT

Erin's a laundry person, Bonnie's a laundry person ... Lana is not. But that's cool, she's a butler's office person, and they're not. With four very active kids (and husband), Bon is forever washing dirty clothes and, as a result, she's always in the laundry. But she actually enjoys this because it gives her a bit of downtime away from her hectic family life. Bonnie likes to think of her laundry room as her own personal space so it has been designed for the person who is in it the most – Bonnie.

HAVE A LITTLE FUN

Remember, a laundry needs to be practical (that's why Bonnie doubled up on appliances and built in loads of storage). But it should also be a place that makes you feel good – somewhere you can express your style.

If you want to do something a little different or exciting design-wise, the splashback is a great place to do this. Bonnie's laundry goes a few steps further – she combined peach, beige and marble tiles in a multitude of different patterns. Not your regular colour scheme but Bonnie loves how that colour combo makes her feel. With a dog-washing tub to boot, this award-winning laundry is definitely one of her favourite rooms in the house.

IS A FLOODED LAUNDRY EVER A GOOD THING?

Yes! But only if it's flooded with natural light. Not only will natural light improve your stain-spotting ability, it will also make the room a more inviting space, help your plants to grow and let in some much-needed fresh air. For an added boost of feel-good sunshine, Bon's laundry also includes a large skylight.

How pampered are these lucky pooches?!

OVERSIZE YOUR MASTER

You've heard the saying 'kitchens sell houses'? Well, this is certainly true. But, in our experience, master bedrooms are definitely a runner-up. Whether you are renovating to sell or creating your forever home, the master is the room the grown-ups (aka the people paying for the house) wake up in every day, and it's a room they should be able to escape to when in need of a sanity check. It really should be a room that makes your jaw drop (in a good way).

GET THOSE PROPORTIONS RIGHT

It's always important to get the proportions of the rooms in a house just right. Having a teeny master bedroom in an acreage house like this would have been a bit weird.

DESIGN A 'CHILD-FREE ZONE', BUT WITH CHILD-FRIENDLY CARPETS

This master suite is definitely a parents' retreat, but a chocolate-covered toddler on a balance bike can be quicker than a stealth ninja, so can a dog with muddy paws. For those reasons, Bon played it safe and chose stain-resistant carpet. Nylon carpet is strong, tough, durable, stain-resistant and cheaper than wool. It's a synthetic fibre that is designed to withstand lots of foot traffic and it comes in loads of colours. It's practical but so soft and luxurious too. Seriously we think it might be the softest carpet we've ever felt. Everyone comments on it.

ANCHOR THE BED

Because Bonnie's room has so many windows, we had to be creative about where to put her bed. In the end, building a freestanding wall was the perfect solution. This way, the stunning four-poster bed faces out towards the French doors and the pool beyond, while the wall creates a walkway into the ensuite from either side. This wall and the ceiling are both fully clad, which adds a gorgeous texture to the room. And of course everything is painted in Bon's couleur du jour, Dulux White on White.

Up close and personal

Don't buy carpet online! You simply must touch, feel and eyeball it in the flesh. Your local store might even let you take a few samples home. If you do, make sure you look at them in different lights. Spend time standing and kneeling on them to check for softness.

WARDROBE GOALS!

At nearly 20 square metres, Bonnie's walk-in-robe area is as big as a decent sized bedroom. But you definitely don't need a huge space to create a dressing area that feels special and luxurious. What really makes this room is the custom hand-made joinery. Add in some stunning gold handles, plush carpet and a built-in bench seat or beautiful stool and you've got a robe made in heaven.

Treat yourself

If you have the floor space, floor-mounted
bath spouts can look spectacular.

Space invaders

Undermount basins take up the least amount of space on the vanity countertop. However, they will steal space from inside the vanity's cupboards and drawers.

CREATE A HOTEL FEEL

Bonnie placed her bath next to her bed with its own bi-fold window, rather than in this ensuite. Having it there, in that nook, creates the 'adults' retreat' feel Bonnie was going for – much like a room in a luxury hotel. If you have the room for a bath in your bedroom and love this idea, you'll need to plan for the costs and labour associated with waterproofing the area around the bathtub.

PLAY UP THE FEELING OF SPACE

Position either a window or a mirror opposite the entry so it is the first thing you see when you walk into the room. You'll get a sense of depth from the view out of the window (assuming it's a good one), or from the reflection in the mirror. But best not to put a mirror and window side-by-side on the same wall as they will actually work against each other. A window will create the illusion of depth, but a mirror reflects something completely different, spoiling the illusion, so they work best on different walls.

THINK BEYOND THE SKYLIGHT

We love a skylight over a shower or bath (or just in general!). If you play your cards right, you might be able to position the skylight so it captures a certain view. Bonnie had the foresight to have a mature palm planted outside just so she could catch glimpses of those green leaves against the blue sky when she showered. #palmtherapy Now that's attention to detail!

Bonnie

"My husband and I always seem to spend quality time talking in our ensuite. Sounds a little bizarre, but with four kids it's sometimes the only place we get time to catch up at the end of the day without life interrupting. I added seating to this ensuite for our evening chats. Beats sitting on the toilet!"

SMALL MOSAIC TILES CAN BE BEAUTIFUL IN A BATHROOM

They're obviously a busier design choice but, done right, they can bring a touch of luxury and a whole lot of wow. These diamond-cut marble mosaics were not only taken up the walls, they were also used across the ceiling in Bonnie's shower, and she loves them because they remind her of little jewels.

PLAN FOR THE YOUNG ADULTS THEY'LL BECOME

Creating a knockout kid's room is a very different styling challenge but it's just as achievable as styling an adult space, and it doesn't have to bust the budget. The focus should be on making the room feel special – a place your child will be happy to be alone in. Don't just design for the child they are now, think ahead to their teenage years – they'll be here sooner than you think! This can be a private space they can escape to, do their homework in, talk on the phone … a well-designed room will be able to grow with them.

BLOCK-OUT BLINDS OR SHUTTERS?

Blinds may not be top of mind when you think about styling a kid's room, but window coverings are key. When they're little, they can help block out the light for those all-important naps. Once your kids are old enough, make sure the curtains or blinds can be opened and closed by your child (to avoid you having to open them every morning). Go cord free, if possible. If you have to have cords, make sure they are within reach but also that they meet safety standards. In these rooms, the plantation shutters are safe and easy-as-pie for little hands to open.

Rock climbing wall

THINK BIGGER BEDS

Most parents buy their kids a standard single bed after they've outgrown their cot, but this is likely to lead to another bed purchase down the track. If the room size is generous enough, consider jumping straight to a king single or even a double.

MAKE IT FUN

Incorporate elements that are a little whimsical, if you can. What little girl or boy can resist a hanging chair! It's magical and fun whether you're six or 16. If you go for this, make sure it's attached to a stud in the ceiling or you'll find it ripped out and lying on the floor! In her oldest son's room, Bonnie even managed to work in a climbing wall under a skylight!

GORGEOUS ART ISN'T JUST FOR GROWN-UPS

Never underestimate how great beautifully framed art can look in your kids' rooms or how much they might appreciate it, even when they're little. Again, think long term when looking for the perfect piece. Remember that you don't have to choose something too childish; something with an element of fun that you both love looking at will be a much better investment.

215

MIX AND MATCH TAPWARE

You don't have to match your tapware across different rooms in the house (unless matching tapware is going to be the common design thread between the rooms). So long as the taps suit the overall style of your home, you can absolutely choose different taps for each bathroom, like Bon did in her home. She used stainless steel, matt white and brass fixtures.

LOOK OUT, NYC SUBWAY! MOVE OVER, LONDON UNDERGROUND ...

The main bathroom sets a new standard in commuter cleanliness. Bon's inspo for this bathroom came from images of a subway station, with its curved ceiling and aptly named subway tiles. Inspiration really is everywhere!

The fun comes not only from the style and colour of the tiles, but also by mixing up the way you lay them. We chose a blue and white combo for these subway tiles and changed up the way they were laid to add more interest. There was no set pattern here, the colour placement was random (oh, the pressure our poor tiler must have felt!).

WEAVE A COMMON DESIGN THREAD THROUGH YOUR BATHROOMS

If you're renovating more than one bathroom in the house, think about tying them all together with a common design thread – for some, that might be the same style of taps, for others it might be a common tile. In this house, marble (or look-alike marble) became that common thread – we used some form of it in every bathroom. In this boys' bathroom, we went for a marble herringbone floor, and in other bathrooms we used little marble penny rounds. Every bathroom has its own unique feature wall and different tapware, but that common thread of marble creates a visual link between them. It also saved on a few extra decision headaches because we were carrying one decision across multiple bathrooms. Nice and simple.

TAKE A (SHOWER) SEAT

A built-in shower seat has been on Erin's wish list for a long time, but Bonnie's beaten her to it. If space allows, who can argue with the luxury and convenience of having a seat to perch on or to rest your leg when shaving? A proper shower seat should be no higher than 500 mm from the floor, and you really need a minimum depth of 250 mm to fit your butt (but 350 mm is better). If you can only squeeze in a depth of 100 mm, it becomes more of a ledge. But this can still be super-handy for shaving legs, just don't fill it up with gooey shampoo bottles – that's what the niche at eye level is for.

WHY SHOULD YOU ORDER YOUR TAPWARE EARLY?

01
The taps you want might have long lead times — especially if they're a special finish.

02
You'll be able to tell your plumber and vanity maker if the taps are coming out of the wall or out of the vanity. #crucial

03
Your plumber will be able to rough in the taps.

White out

We love a matt white tap. They're versatile, and suit a variety of interior styles.

ROUND TILES ARE BEST SERVED IN SMALL PACKAGES

It's hard to resist the little cuties known as penny rounds. Not only do they look great in most styles of bathroom, your tiler might also find them easier to work with as they're much easier to manipulate when creating the necessary fall in your bathroom. They do require lots of grout though, so consider using a stain-resistant epoxy grout, and remember to seal them twice if your roundies are marble.

BATHROOMS NEED STORAGE

Whether that's in or under the vanity, behind the mirror, in a piece of furniture, or all of the above. When drawing up your bathroom layout, think about storage and make sure you create enough to meet the needs of the people using the bathroom. For example, if the bathroom is for kids, a mirrored shaving cabinet may be out of reach for them, so storage down low becomes more important.

A VANITY WITH ZERO STORAGE?

Given our strong feelings about storage, the idea of having zero storage in a vanity might sound crazy. But some people (we're looking at you, Bonnie) are bold enough to do this. Her powder room has nada, zip, zero storage. Why would anyone install a vanity with no storage? Purely for aesthetics. An uninterrupted chunk of stone or timber can pack a pretty punch in a bathroom – especially in a powder room that only gets visited occasionally. And it's possible to provide storage in other places – behind the mirror, perhaps. Some well-chosen floor baskets or shelves can also store towels or toilet paper.

LOCATION, LOCATION, LOCATION

As the 'go-to' bathroom for guests, it's best to build a powder room away from main living spaces like the kitchen and lounge room. Guests don't want their visit to the toilet to happen right under the nose of the homeowners. But equally, you want a powder room to be easily accessible so your visitors aren't having to traipse through your home either. #lanasworstnightmare

ORDER TILES NICE AND EARLY

Long lead times for tiles (especially if they're a bit fancy or imported) are not unusual. Work all the details out 12 weeks before your reno is due to begin to avoid disappointment. (Yes, the prettiest tiles can take that long.)

CREATE THE ULTIMATE OUTDOOR SPACE

If you're on a quest to design the ultimate outdoor entertaining area, we're pretty sure we've found the perfect formula! These five features will help you create an outdoor entertaining space to die for:

01

Put a roof on it. Whether it's to protect you from the scorching summer sun, or to make the space usable even in the pouring rain, a decent covered area is invaluable. A flimsy shade sail just won't cut it compared to a fixed pergola or roof extension that will extend the life of your outdoor area by months each year. Add a wood fire or gas heater to this area

and you've created an extra room that can be used year-round. How gorgeous would it feel to be sitting, rugged up, toasting marshmallows over an outdoor fire while it storms outside?

02

Put your pool in prime position. Even if you're miles from the coast, a pool instantly adds a coastal, resort-like feel to your home. And these days you've got so much choice when it comes to selecting the right pool for your home. Concrete or fibreglass (Lana's choice for her pool on page 90), a light or dark colour, tiled or glass bead, saltwater or mineral water … the options just go on. All of these choices are personal, as is the size of your pool – which will likely be dictated by the size of your outdoor area. Positioning the pool in pride of place in your outdoor area, near the property, will not only give you water views from many spots inside the home, but will also help make sure you get a solid return on your hefty investment by ensuring the pool is used regularly. A pool will keep the kids entertained for hours. And when it's not being used, it doubles as a beautiful water feature. For us, it's the key to feeling you're on holiday at home.

03

Embrace the barbecue. If you think a barbecue should be banished to a back wall, consider this: it's an integral part of outdoor entertaining and incorporating it into an island bench guarantees the chief griller will be included in the action too. A built-in barbecue will help create a seamless look with your outdoor cupboards, and just think what you can fit in the cabinetry underneath – DishDrawer, wine fridge! Pop stools around a barbecue island to create another great area for sitting, chatting, drinking and eating. It's easy to say, 'I'll worry about the barbecue later,' but you really should consider it at the design stage and measure out exactly where it will be placed. If you don't, you could find your alfresco area goes from feeling spacious to small before you can say 'pass the tongs'.

04

Lower the lounge. For a real holiday vibe, a sunken lounge area is the perfect feature. Built-in seating can fit more guests than you may care to host! If you fill those bench seats with luxe, over-sized cushions (made using marine grade outdoor fabric) you'll honestly feel as if you're sitting in a beach club in Ibiza. #mojitoplease! This type of sunken lounge is a perfect place to kick back with a coffee or a cocktail while you watch the kids in the pool.

05

Plant all the palms! Landscaping can make or break the final appearance of your ultimate alfresco area. Without considered planting, your outdoor entertaining area can run the risk of looking stark and unwelcoming. Adding layers of plants and turf does wonders to break up hard surfaces. For a resort-like feel, think massive palms, flowering frangipani and lush green lawns. Now, if only housekeeping would come and wash these pool towels …

FLIP TIP

Don't waste money on an outdoor kitchen unless research of the local area tells you it's a standard expectation.

IS A POOL IN YOUR FUTURE?

If the answer is yes, you'll be happy to know there's one to suit your exact needs. Pool shapes have simplified over the past 15 years. The curvy, freeform styles that were popular in the past have been replaced by the timeless elegance of straight lines. Now, the sophisticated rectangle rules the roost, and because of its popularity you will have the greatest range of fibreglass and concrete pools to choose from. Lana went for a rectangular pool in her backyard, as did Bonnie. But while fibreglass was right for Lana (see page 90), Bonnie went for a concrete pool, as she wanted to customise the pool to her exact specifications.

Watch out!

Have your soil checked before committing to a concrete pool. If the soil is unstable, you could end up with a cracked pool and a broken heart come summer time. In these cases a fibreglass pool is a better choice, as it's able to move with the soil.

THE PROS OF CONCRETE POOLS

01
Look It's hard to beat the look of a concrete pool. There are so many options for surface finishes (pebble, glass bead or tile) that the sky really is the limit when it comes to design.

02
Shape You can make the pool ANY shape you want.

03
Colour You can make the pool ANY colour you want.

04
Add-ons Concrete pools can be customised, so you can add ledges, alcoves and swim-outs wherever you want them.

05
Pool-scaping If you want to create a natural pool-scape with a freeform pool that dovetails beautifully in with your landscape, concrete is the only choice.

06
Waterline tiles These babies sit under the coping (or lip) of your pool, around the surface of the water (hence the name). They add visual interest and also determine the colour that is reflected onto the pool. If your heart is set on using stunning waterline tiles, just be aware that you can only get that premium finish with a concrete pool. If you try to stick them on a fibreglass pool, they might look good from afar, but they'll be far from good up close as they won't sit flush with the shell.

SHALLOW SWIM-OUTS AND LEDGES

Incorporating these special features into your pool design will make it perfect for all ages – grown-ups can chill out half-submerged (with cocktail in hand perhaps?) while toddlers build up their water confidence in those shallow areas. Don't forget to think about the depth of your pool (at both ends) and how it will work for your family. If a concrete pool is your preference, you can custom-build any depth you like, just beware of the extra costs that come with excavating for a super-deep pool. Bon reduced the depth of her deep end for this very reason. #budgetburn

THE CONS OF CONCRETE

There are some downsides to concrete pools. They take longer to install (the concrete has to cure) and they usually cost more because their design can be a little more complex. There's also the ongoing maintenance to think of; most concrete pools need resurfacing every 15 years. Some people also say that concrete pools are inherently colder than fibreglass. Even so, they have many redeeming qualities – complete control over design being one of them.

Easy breezy breezeway

LANDSCAPE DESIGNERS ARE AWESOME!

If your garden is complex, don't be afraid to get some help to work it out, especially if you have multiple levels and lots of 'hardscaping', meaning decks, retaining walls, paving and all that jazz. It's worth investing a few pretty pennies to build the right plan from the start. Bonnie got some help from renowned landscape guru Mon Palmer, and she reckons it's some of the best money she ever spent.

COURTYARD COOL

If you can have gardens not only at the front and back of your home, but also within it, that's a real luxury. Bonnie's sprawling single-storey house is designed with multiple pavilions, and her courtyards create perfect green spaces between them. From almost every window you get glimpses of greenery and this helps bring the outdoors inside.

A BREEZE-WHAAAAT?

Oh yeah, a breezeway. (We didn't know it was called that either before we decided to build one!) It's pretty much a hallway with sliding doors on either side that allow the breeze through. Traditionally, breezeways were undercover walkways leading to a garage or an outdoor shed. But they've crept into modern homes as a gorgeous alternative to a solid hallway. They can also create a beautiful transition between an old house and a new extension. With floor-to-ceiling glass, floaty curtains on either side and beautiful courtyard views, a breezeway can be a really amazing addition to your home and, quite literally, blow your skirt up.

Plant transplant

To save money on plants, look at transplanting some from around your property. We suggest doing a full scope out of your property. Walk around it from corner to corner – you might realise there are plants in your garden you've never seen because they've been covered by weeds or hidden by larger plants.

FAST-TRACK THE LANDSCAPING

Bringing in mature plants means you can skip years of being surrounded by baby saplings and ankle-biting shrubs, and fast-forward to seeing those towering trunks and leaves create an immediate feeling of 'home' like no other. This solution does come at a pretty hefty cost, so you're best to shop around online and see what deals you can find from people getting rid of what you covet. As always, achieving the look you want comes back to proper budgeting and planning right from the beginning of the reno process. If mature plants are on your shopping list, allocate enough money for them early on – and not just for their purchase, but also for transport (which might include a crane) and transplanting costs by landscapers. It's important that mature plants are put in place properly, in areas where their root systems can take hold and where the surrounding plants and environment ensure they have the best chance of thriving.

BUT WAIT, THERE'S MORE!

If you enjoyed this book, you're going to *love* our online Reno School.

The Reno School is an online course created by us to teach you everything we know about how to design, renovate, and style your dream home. We will help you create a vision for your project, understand who you need to work with, how to handle tradies, manage a budget and style a space. We'll show you where to spend versus where to save and how to avoid basic mistakes that can chew up your time, money and happy reno vibes. In a nutshell, it's a much more detailed version of this book, with five times the content! #renogoodness

Whether you're renovating, doing a new build or simply styling a space, you need vision and know-how to get what you want. The Reno School can fast-track your knowledge, build your confidence and get you ready to reno!

Join the thousands of students who have already completed the course and get 10% off with this exclusive discount code – IBOUGHTYOURBOOK

Are you ready to make your dream home a reality?

Visit therenoschool.com today!

Index

Thank you

To Lana, remember four years ago when you said we'd have a book one day and we rolled our eyes? Thank you for never letting our cautious personalities stop you from thinking big and pushing the boundaries.

To the massive legends at Murdoch Books, we know our deadline has come and gone. You patiently waited while we dropped kids at school, dealt with rogue tradies, handled another one of Bonnie's last-minute design changes and let Erin update her never-ending spreadsheet.

To everyone who has helped us with our renos, with running our company, and supported us on our journey (the amazing roller coaster it has been), thank you from the bottom of our hearts. A special shout-out must go to each and every one of our 'followers' whether you've been on the journey for 4 years or just 4 minutes, thanks for making the time and always being so kind and supportive with your messages and emojis. You're the reason we exist.

And most of all, to our families – thanks for letting us chase our dreams. None of this would be possible without your unwavering love, support and coffee.

Erin, Bonnie and Lana
xxx

P.S. Lana, if your grand plans to land us on Ellen's couch actually happen, we promise to stop rolling our eyes.

Murdoch Books wishes to thank the following artists, photographers and suppliers, whose work appears in this book: 30. Art by Anne Harriets; 26 & 30. Photographic print: supplied by OZ Design Furniture; 31, 126, 127. DanielleX; 36, 196, 197, 210. Jai Vasicek; 37. Amelia Anderson; 61 & 67, 69. JJB Photography; 72–3. Supplied by Simple Style Co.; 119. Supplied by Olive et Oriel; 122. Craig McDean (supplied by The Poster Club); 134,135, 138. Supplied by The Print Emporium; 137. Supplied by Urban Road; 144. Karen Jones (supplied by United Interiors); 145. Both prints supplied by United Interiors; 162. Illustration supplied by Inartisan; 164–5, 167, 176. Simon Davidson; 173, 174, 177, 191 Art and skateboard by Lauren Webster; 192. Supplied by OZ Design Furniture; 195. Supplied by A la Mode Studio; 198. Nastia (supplied by Nathan + Jac); 215. Illustration by Libby Watkins; 215. Photographic print by Hugh Holland.

Random husband

Perception vs. reality!

Published in 2019 by Murdoch Books, an imprint of Allen & Unwin
Reprinted 2019 (x4)

Murdoch Books Australia
83 Alexander Street
Crows Nest NSW 2065
Phone: +61 (0)2 8425 0100
Fax: +61 (0)2 9906 2218
murdochbooks.com.au
info@murdochbooks.com.au

Murdoch Books UK
Ormond House
26–27 Boswell Street
London WC1N 3JZ
Phone: +44 (0) 20 8785 5995
murdochbooks.co.uk
info@murdochbooks.co.uk

For Corporate Orders & Custom Publishing, contact our Business Development Team at
salesenquiries@murdochbooks.com.au.

Publisher: Jane Morrow
Editorial Manager: Katie Bosher
Creative Direction: northwoodgreen.com
Principal photographer: Monique Easton
Illustrator: Sophie Bell
Production Director: Lou Playfair